ACTIVITIES FOR TEACHING CITIZENSHIP IN SECONDARY SCHOOLS

David Turner and Patricia Baker

KOGAN PAGE

First published in 2000 by Kogan Page Limited

Kogan Page Limited
120 Pentonville Road
London N1 9JN
UK

British Library Cataloguing in Publication Data

A CIP record for this book is available from the British Library.

ISBN 0 7494 33442

Typeset by D & N Publishing, Baydon, Wiltshire
Printed and bound in Great Britain by Thanet Press Ltd, Margate

CONTENTS

ACKNOWLEDGEMENTS

David Turner and Patricia Baker wish to express their heartfelt thanks to all the people who contributed ideas and materials for use in this book. Without their help and assistance, freely and willingly given, this book would never have seen the light of day. The list is a long one and includes a large number of the staff at Wellsway School:

Paul Kent for allowing the project to go ahead in the school, and for his support and advice that helped us to manage the extra burden that contributing to this book made to already hard-pressed teachers.

Special thanks must go to Clarissa Moncrieff who not only contributed the English and some of the PSHE (Personal, Social and Health Education) lessons but who also took a keen interest in the whole book and made a number of invaluable suggestions.

Anna Barker who gave an insight into the relationship between citizenship and key skills.

Max Harvey who contributed the Key Stage 3 drama lessons and gave an insight into the role of drama within other areas, Guy Martin who contributed the Key Stage 4 drama lessons and John Smith for help and advice on Key Stage 4 drama.

Ian Tanner who contributed the section linking work experience and citizenship.

Jan Helps who gave material for the role of the Internet.

Diana Allez and Peter Baker who contributed some of the PSHE lessons.

June Breese who contributed the art lessons and Roy Page who contributed the music lessons.

Louise Riddoch, Debbie Barker, Rod Bell and Carl Bennett who were the authors of Chapter 15.

Karen Frost who contributed the geography lessons for Chapter 8.

Pauline Culshaw who contributed to Chapter 9 and helped to draw the links between history and citizenship.

Shaun Wainwright who contributed the design and technology lessons.

Tina Tabor who contributed the maths lessons at Key Stage 4 and Shirley Elder who gave up time to explain the content of the maths weekend and generously allowed her work to form the basis of a section of this book. Shirley Anderson who contributed the Key Stage 3 maths lessons and gave us an insight into citizenship and Key Skills within maths.

Linda Hall who contributed Chapter 11.

Jacqui Pannet for generously sharing her ideas and time.

Roy Lofkin who contributed the modern language lessons.

Veronica Northam who contributed the Key Stage 4 business lesson and the case studies on using the Internet.

Dave Sage who contributed the Key Stage 3 science lessons and Nick Glossop who contributed the Key Stage 4 science lessons.

Lastly special thanks must go to Peter Baker, Patricia's husband, who acted as a critical friend and who had to put the children to bed far more often than was, strictly, his turn and to Poppy Turner, David's wife, whose original idea this was and who spent a lot of time copy typing, proofing, checking the text for sanity and keeping the whole project on track.

PREFACE

The recent introduction of the concept of citizenship into schools is no great innovation to many teachers who are already addressing similar issues in daily lessons or during tutor group and PSHE lessons. However, citizenship has now been more clearly defined and many teachers will find themselves faced with having to deliver lessons on and around the citizenship agenda for the first time.

This book is intended to be a dip-in resource for school managers and teachers at Key Stages 3 and 4. It is hoped that it will be useful both as a source of ready made relevant material and as a thought promoter. Many of the activities in the book can be amended and extended in a variety of different ways and the methods suggested can be adapted for use with different content.

The book is aimed at the classroom teacher who will have to teach citizenship issues, either in PSHE classes or in mainstream curriculum lessons. It is one of two books that are intended to be stand-alone resources. The other book, *Developing Citizenship in Secondary Schools*, is addressed to the management team of a school who wish to provide wide scale opportunities for learning in the citizenship arena within the whole school or larger (eg whole year) groups. This second book *Activities for Teaching Citizenship in Secondary Schools* has some ideas for the use of more generic methods in Part 1 and is set out under subject headings in Part 2. The two books together provide a flexible and easily accessible source of ideas for use in a wide range of situations.

The books are the result of a collaboration between an independent management consultant, David Turner, who is the author of a book of role play resources for management trainers, and members of the teaching staff at Wellsway School in Keynsham, near Bristol, led by Patricia Baker, the Deputy Head Teacher at the school. The material presented here is either directly derived from activities already tried and tested in the school or developed for the purpose and classroom tested for the books.

In common with many schools, Wellsway is adamant that there is no need to respond to every new initiative by setting up complex structures and new working parties. Enough demands are placed upon education and educators without the profession adding more to the workload. Thus, when some new requirement comes over the horizon, the first response is to see what is already being done in that area under some other guise.

At Wellsway, after having looked at the guidelines for citizenship, we felt pretty confident that we had some good things already going on in that area. Many other schools must also feel this and sharing good practice between schools is important. It not only spreads examples of 'things that work' but also cuts down on the workload of teachers. As a school we wanted to share our expertise and we are also grateful for information which comes our way.

What then did we have going on which contributed, or could contribute, towards the implementation of citizenship? The following might give a flavour:

- In the interest of continuity and progression, tutors remain with the same tutor group (unless promotion or something similar intervenes!) throughout Years 7–11. This gives tutors a wonderful opportunity to get to know their tutees well throughout the course of their school careers. The tutees also get to know their tutors well. This relationship is crucially important as the pupils progress through the school and many of the demands of citizenship can be addressed through this relationship within the pastoral system.

- There was an existing delivery of PSHE material by tutors to their tutor groups. The PSHE programme is one that already delivers many of the requirements of citizenship. It is devised by year teams who arrange a handover of materials at the end of each year. Thus, the material delivered by Year 9 tutors is handed on to the Year 8 tutors (who may well adapt it, but the body of the work is there) at the end of the academic year, and at the same time the Year 9 tutors receive the materials used by the Year 10 team and so on.

- A training day is built into the school calendar for the handover of materials. In this way, time is made available for discussion and development of work. We no longer have the feeling that we used to have that, although PSHE is valued, no time was made available for it.

■ There were a number of events already established and built in to the school calendar and these major events are arranged so that they do not conflict. This means that there is not too much stress placed on any group of pupils, students or staff at any one time. These events include a number of those described within the two books such as the fashion show, the philosophy and belief day, work experience, school drama productions, activities week, the maths weekend and the work of the environmental group.

■ We have created a strong feeling of pupil power in its best sense, ie a recognition by pupils that their opinions and suggestions are sought and valued. Pupils will not always get their own way but it is important that if their suggestions or requests cannot be accommodated (for whatever reason) a full and logical explanation is given. The work of the Year and School Councils and the suggestions from tutor groups or individual pupils are taken seriously if they are forwarded through the appropriate channels. Examples include such areas as lunchtime arrangements, seating/social areas and the Buddy System. These and others are described in *Developing Citizenship in Secondary Schools* by the same authors.

■ There is a 'can do' philosophy within the school body. Possibly this arises out of the sense of pupil power, but it appears in different guises. It has been seen in the work of some Year 10 pupils which resulted in changes to the school uniform, in the brainchild and hard work of one student that resulted in a whole new support system being established, in the sheer hard work of a group who put on the fashion show and in the voice of one Year 7 pupil who suggested a look at the standard of food provided in the school canteen. This positive attitude is already in evidence in many areas and bodes well for the citizens of tomorrow.

■ A thriving publication, 'The Ammonite', which goes out each week to pupils and parents. As an aid to communication it is invaluable. It tells pupils, students and parents what is going on within the school community. It celebrates successes, it has published individual pieces of work and has provided solace and support in times of sadness. It relates to our school and the wider community; it is citizenship in action.

■ We have the Wellsway Community Development Group which is spearheading a Lottery Bid in order to provide a sports centre for the community. This is bringing together parents, pupils, teachers, governors and local businesses in an effort to improve facilities for a wide cross section of people.

Many schools have these or similar things in operation. We must use them to help our introduction of citizenship. We felt that we had something to offer and these books are the result.

With apologies to Terry Waite CBE, quoted on page 13 of *Citizenship, The National Curriculum for England*, (www.nc.uk.net), who said 'It is only when you know how to be a citizen of your own country that you can learn how to be a citizen of the world', we believe that being a citizen of your own school is invaluable in learning to become a citizen of your own country.

HOW TO USE THIS BOOK

We believe that the material suggested in this book provides activities and approaches that can be used very flexibly to cover subject specific, key skills and citizenship learning. The activities set out in this volume are focussed towards teaching citizenship in the classroom across the curriculum (but will also undoubtedly be applicable in the transfer of key skills) while those in *Developing Citizenship in Secondary Schools*, the sister volume to this book, are aimed more at school managers and large-scale activities.

The book is organized into chapters that put forward ideas for different activities. In Part 1, chapter 1 explains the requirements of citizenship and chapter 2 is a look at the management issues surrounding the introduction of citizenship teaching. Chapter 3 looks at some generic methods of teaching citizenship. In Part 2, chapters 4 to 16 cover a range of single lessons or schemes of lessons that can be used to teach citizenship alongside the individual subjects.

Use of activities

The most important thing to ensure the successful introduction of citizenship within a school is to take stock. The school and each department or faculty will need to see what is already in existence and can be developed, made more explicit, relevant, enhanced or used in another way rather than building a whole new set of activities and materials. Any gaps or deficiencies can then be identified and set in place to meet the requirements of citizenship at Key Stages 3 and 4. It is important that, as with any development, there is a sense of ownership. This does not mean that every school has to start from scratch. Co-operation and learning from each other is important in the classroom and also at a management level. This book and the activities described should provide a starting point for that learning. Within this context, the best people to know what needs to be done are the staff themselves, working within departments, faculties and year teams.

Schools have different strengths and priorities, each serves a different area with a different cultural background and so the activities described will not always be of direct relevance. Therefore the activities in this book, and its companion volume, are ones that give ideas and pointers as well as providing specific material. They are not intended to be prescriptive. They may be lifted directly from the page and put into practice in the school or in the classroom or used as templates for a wide range of similar activities which individual schools and teachers can create to meet their own teaching and learning goals more closely. If, as we hope, the book and its material appeal to teachers it will be useful both as a dip-in resource and as a prompt, or thought starter, for more different activities and lessons.

In all the activities described in this book there is an implicit requirement for the teacher to ensure that the lessons for citizenship are made clear. In the course of discussions, as a response to questions or as part of the normal delivery of the lesson there will be many and varied opportunities to clarify an issue or make a point that will extend the pupils' knowledge of citizenship. These opportunities should be grasped as they appear, whether or not the lesson has as one of its aims some part of the citizenship curriculum. However, where the lesson does have such an aim it becomes even more important to seize the opportunity to provide additional clarification or learning whenever possible.

Not every subject will readily address all the aspects of citizenship contained in the curriculum but almost every subject will be able to raise issues of citizenship from time to time, either as a conscious intention or because the opportunity arises. Just as a good parent will seize the opportunity to push home a lesson about safety or honesty when it arises, so teachers should be alert to the opportunity to draw lessons for citizenship.

It will never be possible, in a book like this, to foresee each and every one of the learning outcomes that may emerge from a lesson and we anticipate that there will be many more beneficial outcomes than those that we have specifically listed under each activity. Equally, depending on the nature and direction of some of the discussion, it may not always prove possible to extract all of those that we have listed.

Drawing as we have from a large number of people, the material in this book inevitably appears with some differences in format and structure but we believe that we have maintained a consistent standard for that material.

PART 1

BACKGROUND INFORMATION

In this part we set out to provide information about citizenship and its introduction as a curriculum subject into the school, and to provide some thoughts on generic methods that can be used across the curriculum.

Chapter 1 describes citizenship and provides relevant extracts from the government document on the subject. Chapter 2 addresses some management issues and gives some thoughts about how to go about implementing its teaching. Chapter 3 looks at useful generic methods of teaching that can be used anywhere in the curriculum to support learning about citizenship.

CHAPTER 1

WHAT IS CITIZENSHIP?

This chapter sets out the citizenship requirements upon which the rest of the book is based. It is, therefore, written in a rather different style from the rest of the book which is intended to be a practical, dip-in resource for the teacher. This chapter, by contrast, is necessarily based closely on the concise definition of citizenship used by the DfEE in the National Curriculum. We make no apology for this; it is essential to understand the requirement before trying to teach pupils something about their roles and duties as citizens. The full document can be obtained from the National Curriculum Web site on www.nc.uk.net

Background

The report of the Advisory Group on Education for Citizenship and the Teaching of Democracy was delivered in September 1998. It recommended that the teaching of citizenship and democracy become a statutory requirement on schools. It identified three principal dimensions: participation in democracy, the responsibilities and rights of a citizen and the value of community activity. The acceptance of this report by government has led to the development of a detailed citizenship curriculum for schools. This becomes mandatory in September 2002.

Citizenship and the National Curriculum

In their forward to *Citizenship: The National Curriculum for England*, published in 1999, the Right Honourable David Blunkett, Secretary of State for Education and Employment and Sir William Stubbs, Chairman of the Qualifications and Curriculum Authority, refer to the equality of opportunity that underpins the school curriculum and of a commitment to valuing ourselves, our families and other relationships, the wider groups to which we belong, the diversity in our society and the environment in which we live.

The National Curriculum determines what should be taught in our schools and sets attainment targets for learning so that everyone has a shared understanding of the skills and knowledge that pupils should gain from their time in school. From September 2002 the curriculum will include citizenship. The aim is to provide pupils with an understanding of their roles and responsibilities as citizens in a modern democracy and so help them to deal with difficult moral and social questions that arise in their lives and in society.

Citizenship teaching, along with personal, social and health education (PSHE), is intended to give pupils the knowledge, skills and understanding to play an effective role in society at local, national and international levels. It should promote their spiritual, moral, social and cultural development and help them to live confident, healthy, independent lives, as individuals, parents, workers and members of society.

The programmes of study set out what pupils should be taught and the attainment targets set out the expected standards of pupils' performance. Programmes of study for Key Stages 3 and 4 are reproduced below.

In both cases citizenship teaching should ensure that knowledge and understanding about becoming informed citizens are acquired and applied when developing skills of enquiry and communication, and participation and responsible action.

PROGRAMME OF STUDY FOR CITIZENSHIP AT KEY STAGE 3

KNOWLEDGE AND UNDERSTANDING ABOUT BECOMING INFORMED CITIZENS

Pupils should be taught about:

- the legal and human rights and responsibilities underpinning society, basic aspects of the criminal justice system, and how both relate to young people;

- the diversity of national, regional, religious and ethnic identities in the United Kingdom and the need for mutual respect and understanding;

continued

continued

- central and local government, the public services they offer and how they are financed, and the opportunities to contribute;

- the key characteristics of parliamentary and other forms of government;

- the electoral system and the importance of voting;

- the work of community-based, national and international voluntary groups;

- the importance of resolving conflict fairly;

- the significance of the media in society;

- the world as a global community, and the political, economic, environmental and social implications of this, and the role of the European Union, the Commonwealth and the United Nations.

DEVELOPING SKILLS OF ENQUIRY AND COMMUNICATION

Pupils should be taught to:

- think about topical political, spiritual, moral, social and cultural issues, problems and events by analysing information and its sources, including ICT-based sources;

- justify orally and in writing a personal opinion about such issues, problems or events;

- contribute to group and exploratory class discussions, and take part in debates.

DEVELOPING SKILLS OF PARTICIPATION AND RESPONSIBLE ACTION

Pupils should be taught to:

- use their imagination to consider other people's experiences and be able to think about, express and explain views that are not their own;

- negotiate, decide and take part responsibly in both school and community-based activities;

- reflect on the process of participating.

PROGRAMME OF STUDY FOR CITIZENSHIP AT KEY STAGE 4

KNOWLEDGE AND UNDERSTANDING ABOUT BECOMING INFORMED CITIZENS

Pupils should be taught about:

- the legal and human rights and responsibilities underpinning society and how they relate to citizens, including the role and operation of the criminal and civil justice systems;

- the origins and implications of the diverse national, regional, religious and ethnic identities in the United Kingdom and the need for mutual respect and understanding;

- the work of parliament, government and the courts in making and shaping the law;

- the importance of playing an active part in democratic and electoral processes;

- how the economy functions, including the role of business and financial services;

- the opportunities for individuals and voluntary groups to bring about social change locally, nationally, in Europe and internationally;

- the importance of a free press, and the media's role in society, including the Internet, in providing information and affecting opinion;

- the rights and responsibilities of consumers, employers and employees;

- the United Kingdom's relations in Europe, including the European Union, and relations with the Commonwealth and the United Nations;

- the wider issues and challenges of global interdependence and responsibility, including sustainable development and Local Agenda 21.

continued

continued

DEVELOPING SKILLS OF ENQUIRY AND COMMUNICATION

Pupils should be taught to:

- research a topical political, spiritual, moral, social or cultural issue, problem or event by analysing information from different sources, including ICT-based sources, showing an awareness of the use and abuse of statistics;

- express, justify and defend orally and in writing a personal opinion about such issue, problems or events;

- contribute to group and exploratory class discussions, and take part in formal debates.

DEVELOPING SKILLS OF PARTICIPATION AND RESPONSIBLE ACTION

Pupils should be taught to:

- use their imagination to consider other people's experiences and be able to think about, express, explain and critically evaluate views that are not their own;

- negotiate, decide and take part responsibly in school and community-based activities;

- reflect on the process of participating.

Attainment targets

The types and range of performance that pupils should be able to demonstrate at the end of the key stages are broadly similar. For Key Stage 3 they are:

Pupils have a broad knowledge and understanding of the topical events they study; the rights, responsibilities and duties of citizens; the role of the voluntary sector; forms of government; provision of public services and the criminal and legal systems. They show how the public gets information and how opinion is formed and expressed, including through the media. They show understanding of how and why changes take place in society. Pupils take part in school- and community-based activities, demonstrating personal and group responsibility in their attitudes to themselves and others.

Key Stage 4 differs only in the depth of understanding required. A 'comprehensive' knowledge and understanding is required. In addition, pupils are required to obtain and use information from different sources. They also need to reflect on and critically evaluate what they learn and what they do.

Table 1.1. Summary of programmes of study for citizenship at Key Stages 3 and 4

Knowledge and understanding

Key Stage 3	Key Stage 4
Legal and human rights and responsibilities	Legal and human rights and responsibilities
Basic aspects of the criminal justice system	Operation of the criminal and civil justice systems
The diversity of national, regional, religious and ethnic identities in the UK	The origins and implications of the diverse national, regional, religious and ethnic identities in the UK
Central and local government public services	
Parliamentary and other forms of government	The work of parliament, government and the courts in making law
The electoral system and voting	The electoral system and democratic process
Voluntary groups (community, national and international)	How individuals and voluntary groups can influence society
Conflict resolution	
Media in society	Media in society and the Internet

continued

continued

The world as a global community (EU, UN, Commonwealth)	Global interdependence and sustainable development (Local Agenda 21)
	The UK's relations in Europe and with the Commonwealth and UN
	How the economy functions, the role of business and financial services
	The rights and responsibilities of consumers, employers and employees

Skills of enquiry and communication

Key Stage 3	Key Stage 4
Think and analyse information about topical issues, problems and events	Research and analyse information about topical issues, problems and events
Analyse information from ICT-based sources	Analyse information from different sources including ICT-based sources
Justify a personal opinion orally and in writing	Express, defend and justify a personal opinion orally and in writing
Contribute to group and class discussion	Contribute to group and class discussion
Take part in debates	Take part in formal debates

Skills of participation and responsible action

Key Stage 3	Key Stage 4
Use imagination to consider other people's experiences	Use imagination to consider other people's experiences
Think about, express and explain views that are not their own	Think about, express and explain and critically evaluate views that are not their own
Negotiate, decide and take part responsibly in school- and community-based activities	Negotiate, decide and take part responsibly in school- and community-based activities
Reflect on the process of participation	Reflect on the process of participation

CHAPTER 2

MANAGEMENT ISSUES

Teaching citizenship should not, we believe, become a mountain for schools to climb. However, realistically there will need to be some changes to the way things are done. The key areas for consideration include:

- introducing/consolidating citizenship into the curriculum;
- the links to key skills;
- resources;
- staff development;
- stakeholders – governors, parents, etc.

These we will examine in turn.

Introducing/consolidating citizenship into the curriculum

There will need to be a well-managed process to introduce or consolidate the teaching of citizenship in the school if it is to become an effective and all-inclusive part of the school's activities. Like any change, the introduction of these new ideas will need to be managed. The management of change can be difficult and there can be pain.

There are several implementation issues that should be considered when trying to introduce citizenship in a systematic way or to consolidate what is already being done. These are likely to be:

- managing yet another initiative or 'initiative fatigue';

- the cross-curricular challenge;

- the incorporation of existing good practice within the school.

Managing another initiative

Most schools will have agreed aims for the conduct of their activities. These will have been arrived at in a variety of different ways but most schools will have agreed their aims through discussion and negotiation amongst pupils/students/staff/parents/governors. By the very nature of the constitution of the governing body, that discussion will have brought in the views of the wider community. Where there has been such involvement from a wide cross-section of people, there will be a commitment to achieving these aims from a whole community who will all be working towards the same end. Therefore, citizenship is already likely to have been accepted as an integral part of what the school is trying to achieve. This will manifest itself in some or all of the following or similar aims:

- to enable all young people to achieve their full potential academically, emotionally, physically and spiritually;

- to foster the development of personal moral values;

- to develop a sense of self-esteem and the habits of self-discipline;

- to promote creative and aesthetic awareness and enjoyment;

- to develop a wide range of skills in communication;

- to develop respect for other people and the environment and an awareness of rights and responsibilities;

- to encourage active citizenship – participation in decision-making and the democratic process;

- to educate young people to respect and value other cultures and to be aware of issues relating to the wider community;

- to foster positive links with the local community;

- to educate for and practise equality of opportunity;

- to prepare young people effectively for the demands of a rapidly changing high-technology society;

- to promote a healthy lifestyle;

- to encourage independent life-long learning.

The introduction of the teaching of citizenship can be directly compared and aligned with the teaching of key skills and can be seen as another, cross-curricular, layer or learning stream to complement and enhance what is already being done in the classroom. Rather than being seen as a whole new subject area it should be viewed as a way of approaching a more holistic view of education and a route towards more 'joined-up' teaching

It will be important, in order to gain commitment and ownership, to involve staff in the process and encourage them to develop material within their own subject specialism which will facilitate the drawing out of subject-specific, key skills and citizenship lessons. Planning time should be made available for these activities. Availability of such time will be limited but it is suggested that INSET time be set aside for departments to develop their own approaches and materials. We hope that this book and its sister volume *Developing Citizenship in Secondary Schools* will seed and inform that thinking while providing a versatile bank of material and ideas for use.

The cross-curricular challenge

With increasing emphasis being placed on results, and the measurement of results being a key performance indicator, it is inevitable that departments will wish to concentrate on delivery of the National Curriculum since results in that area will be the primary measure of their performance. However, there are distinct pressures from government, and therefore from OFSTED, to deliver rounded education in a more 'joined-up' fashion. The key skills approach is an example, citizenship is another.

Figure 2.1 below shows the relationships between various activities in schools and it is clear that the obstacles to effective cross-curricular working will appear between departments. Therefore, the impact of citizenship as an extra burden must be reduced and we believe that this is best done through the use of activities and materials that will encourage concurrent learning in all three fields – subject, key skills and citizenship.

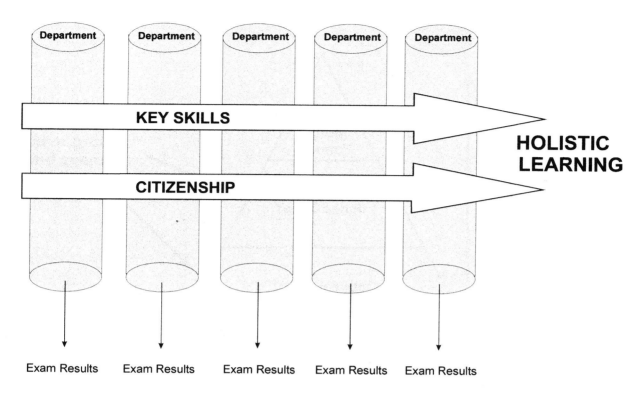

Figure 2.1 The relationship between various school activities

The incorporation of existing good practice within the school

It is very likely that every school will already be doing things, as part of PSHE lessons or elsewhere, that will contribute to the needs of citizenship teaching and it would be a great shame if these were to be abandoned in some flurry of enthusiastic new activity. It is essential for departments to audit or take stock of their materials and methods to see just how much or how little new material needs to be incorporated. Minimizing the extra workload must be a priority. The audit approach will help to do that and it should also give recognition to those who have developed good material that can be copied and shared. A small group of champions, led perhaps by the PSHE department if there is one, could control such an audit and ensure that existing good practice is recognized and shared, and that the effort of origination and development of activities is not duplicated in different departments. Often ideas in one subject area are easily translated into another without the need for prolonged creative thought. INSET time can also be used for this process of sharing good practice.

The links to key skills

The key skills area is one that already has a high profile at Key Stage 5. Key Stage 5 key skills qualification is worth up to 60 UCAS points. In order for students to reach this high level it is vital that they develop both the key skills and a cross-curricular approach to learning at Key Stages 3 and 4. The post-16 changes, implemented in September 2000, emphasize the importance of communication, working with others, application of number, information technology, problem-solving and improving one's own learning alongside A levels and other courses. These areas form an integral part of the curriculum and have obvious links with citizenship at Key Stages 3 and 4. As such, key skills and citizenship can be seen as mutually supportive, each feeding the other. There is, or can be, a symbiotic relationship between citizenship and key skills. Some schools are already recognising and/or accrediting key skills both at Key Stage 4 and Key Stage 5. Methods of doing this vary. Key skills can, for example, be recognized and identified at the end of a particular course or piece of work, or there may be an input to give pupils the opportunity to demonstrate key skills – a project for example, which could be teacher guided or supported self-study. Citizenship could be used here. It could be a vehicle for demonstrating key skills or key skills could be used as research aids. Taking this model a stage further, if key skills are recognized or accredited then so too could citizenship. To minimize the workload, an area or areas of citizenship and an area of key skills could be negotiated with each department. They then develop an activity to cover both and fulfil the requirements to gain key skills accreditation.

Resources

Co-ordination of the approach

It would be very easy for each department/area in a school to carry out an audit and simply tick boxes. For example, if a history department at Key Stage 3 looks at the development of 'universal suffrage' it can claim it has 'done' democracy. As all Key Stage 3 teachers teach this element then all teachers too have 'done' democracy and so have all Key Stage 3 pupils. Wrong! There is an issue of co-ordination within the department to ensure all teachers put the information in the context of the twenty-first century to show its importance to citizens of today, perhaps in the light of rights and responsibilities. This can be achieved quite easily by formal or informal discussion at department meetings or elsewhere. Time must be set aside for departments to address the contribution they can, or could, make to citizenship. For most departments we suggest there should be 'obvious' areas and guidelines are available to help in this. However, a whole-school approach should help identify and plan the time available and give clear guidelines for departments to use (see 'Staff development' below).

Co-ordination across departments

It is always useful to know what other departments are doing so that good practice can be shared. To re-teach something which has been covered elsewhere is a waste of valuable time. Using what has been taught elsewhere can be built upon to help pupils make connections and break down barriers between subjects or 'de-compartmentalize' them. For citizenship this is even more important. Co-ordination across departments is difficult and could be very time-consuming so a simple list of the topics addressed in each year or across a key stage by each subject area could be published. A year planner in a year office or in the staff-room could be utilized to display the topics under discussion in each area. Teachers straying into areas of possible overlap are, therefore, forewarned and can discuss with their colleagues what has been covered and in which way.

Overview of the subject

Unlike departmental schemes of work, which are regularly reviewed at departmental meetings (through common assessment and testing and through shared discussions), it is much less easy to have an overview of a cross-curricular topic. It may be appropriate for the key skills and/or PSHE co-ordinators within a school to take responsibility for the overview of citizenship teaching as there are so many obvious links with these subjects. Another possibility is for an existing team or working party to extend its brief. Citizenship could fit easily within a guidance review team or a careers guidance orbit, or it might become a significant part of the responsibilities of pastoral heads of Key Stage 3 and Key Stage 4. The important point is that there will need to be a whole-school overview of citizenship activity within the school and existing structures should be used wherever possible, rather than new or specifically created working parties or groups, to carry out this function.

Ensuring universal coverage

At Key Stage 3, all pupils will have access to citizenship teaching through PSHE and within subject areas. Thus it is safe to assume that, providing the aspects of co-ordination and overview discussed above have been addressed, all pupils will have been taught citizenship. At Key Stage 4, however, because not all pupils follow the same curriculum, this is not the case. All pupils do, however, study English, maths, science, a modern foreign language, a technology subject and religious education. Most schools have a PSHE programme in place and this can be modified to address significant areas. To ensure that all Key Stage 4 pupils will have access to citizenship teaching there will be a greater onus on teachers in those subject areas to consider citizenship in their lessons. This issue will need to be addressed by the school and Key Stage 4 co-ordinators to ensure equality of access.

Staff development

Awareness and recognition of achievements to date

This is a very important first step in the process of the introduction or consolidation of citizenship teaching and of the audit which is so important to answer the question 'Where are we now?' Many departments will already have begun to look at their involvement in citizenship. Perhaps there has already been work done in this area under a different guise – equal opportunities, for example, or some aspect of the legacy of TVEI (Technical and Vocational Education Initiative) in which schools were encouraged to look at political awareness, at work-related activities and at education for industrial understanding. The legacy from some of these initiatives, with subsequent development, could quite easily feed into citizenship. Time spent reflecting on what has already been achieved is time well spent. This reflection will de-mystify and improve the general understanding of what citizenship really means. It will recognize the work done and raise the profile of relevant activities and in so doing will reassure the staff that citizenship is not necessarily some huge mountain to climb; teams will probably discover that they are already well on the way up the slope.

Attitudes/departmental myopia

It is understandable that the priority of every department will be teaching their specific subject. Standard attainment tests at Key Stage 3 and GCSE results, not to mention league tables, dictate this. It is well known that departments never have enough time but some must be made available to ensure that the necessary audits and re-direction of resources can and do occur. A whole-school approach is the best way of making sure this time is made available. Thus all departments, at their next departmental meeting, could be required to have a specific 'citizenship' agenda or time could be made available for departments to discuss specific citizenship issues on a training day.

Once time has been made available, the first barrier for all to overcome is the mind-set that suggests citizenship is an additional burden to a teacher or that it is an area which 'other departments' can/should address (the inference being 'but not us'). Some subject areas, like business studies and history for example, might more naturally assimilate the citizenship agenda than others. However, all areas can contribute, utilizing their existing schemes of work. Within a school, it would be very helpful if a specific individual (eg the PSHE co-ordinator, Key Stage 3 co-ordinator, key skills co-ordinator), who has attended courses relating to citizenship and is part of the co-ordinating team or structure within the school, is able to make an input into different departments if difficulties are perceived.

Use of INSET days

The culture of the school will best indicate the format of a training day. It may be appropriate to invite input from an external 'expert' or, alternatively, to provide home-grown material. Either approach, or indeed a mix of the two, has merit but in any event this really is a situation in which the much talked about 'sense of ownership' is vitally important.

Suggestions for inclusion in such a training day could include the following:

■ Compilation of achievements to date within the context of citizenship and recognition of them. This would help to develop a checklist of useful activities. An example is shown below. This could be achieved by:

> *– discussion by a team of a pre-prepared list, perhaps the staff development team, curriculum team, PSHE team etc;*
>
> *– brainstorming to create a list on the day using information from all colleagues. This could then be put into a semblance of order and distributed following the training day;*
>
> *– convening small groups, either subject based or cross-curricular, to work together to assemble ideas and then share them in a plenary session.*

■ Input from 'an expert' or someone within the school showing how citizenship can be an integral part of a lesson. Within any school there will be departments which are already more in tune/comfortable with the ideas and concepts of citizenship. Arranging for someone who has already adopted good practice in the teaching of citizenship to present their ideas to the rest of their colleagues is a superb professional development opportunity and a chance for departments to share their expertise with others. Depending upon the people involved, strategies might include:

> *– use of overhead projector; a lesson plan talked through;*
>
> *– sharing of resources, looking at how one particular aspect of the lesson has been addressed;*
>
> *– identifying pupils' work where citizenship has clearly made an impact.*

■ A variation on the above might be to use the same approach but have colleagues from more than one department who have collaborated/are collaborating on a particular issue present the lessons from their experience.

■ An input from the key skills co-ordinator, or another member of staff with a specific interest in this area, to talk through and demonstrate the links between key skills and citizenship. One way of doing this might be to show, for example, how using ICT skills can produce a series of graphs, spreadsheets, charts and so on, to support work on local government and elections. If the

> Whichever way the audit is approached, or whichever strategies are employed, the end result should be threefold:
>
> - All teachers are more comfortable with issues within the citizenship umbrella.
>
> - Departments start or continue sharing information.
>
> - All teachers are aware of the wide variety of whole-school activities addressing citizenship issues that are going on in their school so that appropriate links can be made.

finished product was to be presented to a class by the pupil(s) involved, then more key skills targets are met alongside the greater understanding of this aspect of citizenship.

- Time made available for departments to think about how they would address a particular topic within the citizenship remit. If this were a time-limited exercise there could be the opportunity for two or three groups to give a brief presentation on their work.

- Alternatively, make time available for the same purpose to cross-curricular groups.

Stakeholders

There are two significant stakeholder groups, governors and parents. The role of each is described below.

Governors

The introduction/amplification of citizenship in the curriculum for Key Stage 3 and Key Stage 4 will clearly have implications for the governing body. The governors' curriculum committee or its equivalent will need to be kept aware of developments and also be kept informed of the method of delivery. It may be that a particular governor would want to be, or could be encouraged to be, the 'link' governor.

The governing body, however, could play a more active and involved role in citizenship. Many schools are fortunate enough to have governors who are

EXAMPLE: ACTIVITIES AIDING THE TEACHING OF CITIZENSHIP

A possible checklist of activities identified or generated to help the systematic introduction or consolidation of the teaching of citizenship within the school could include:

THE SUBJECT AUDIT	The first step to answering 'Where are we now?'
PSHE AUDIT	A way of addressing any areas not covered in specific subjects
KEY SKILLS AUDIT	Each school probably already has a method of accrediting/assessing key skills
CAREERS CALENDAR CHECKLIST, ESPECIALLY AT KEY STAGE 4	Most schools already deliver work experience placements (one or two weeks) and may also offer opportunities for work shadowing and interview experience
'SPECIALIST' DAYS OR CONFERENCES	These can take a variety of formats and can be used at Key Stage 3 or Key Stage 4. Areas which could be addressed are industry day, religious education/philosophy and belief conference, environmental awareness day, mock elections
EXTRA CURRICULAR ACTIVITIES	Plays with a specific message, debating societies and debating forum, charity collections and support for charities, field trips, Duke of Edinburgh Award
SPECIFIC ACTIVITIES	School and/or year council, Young Enterprise, 'Buddy' system, foreign exchanges/visits
WORKING WITH OUTSIDE AGENCIES	Bank set up within the school, support for charities, assemblies used as a platform for organizations, eg Relate, AL Anon and Alateen, Childline, Cruse, etc.
OTHERS	Study days, activities week, presentation evenings

The above list is by no means exhaustive but it gives a flavour of the many and diverse activities that already occur in most schools and which already make a contribution to the teaching of citizenship. Most of these topics are covered in later chapters of this book.

currently in or recently retired from industry, local government, legal or other relevant professions. Consequently, they have much knowledge, many skills and useful contacts. They may also have time available. As governors they have already shown commitment to the school and some may well wish to express this commitment further and use their expertise to support citizenship teaching.

We suggest a number of ways in which this expertise can be used:

■ Involvement in mock interviews for Key Stage 4 pupils. Depending upon the time available, these can include a number of elements. The mock interview could mirror exactly a real situation with a job advert, letter of application, interview and a realistic debrief. If time does not permit, it could be a less-demanding exercise with a more general situation discussing interview techniques. The more realistic the situation can be made, the more effective it will be.

■ Use of contacts to create situations which give pupils a deeper understanding of the wider community. These can be many and varied. For Key Stage 4 pupils for example, groups could be involved in a design project with a local firm, work shadowing could be set up with a variety of occupations or a group could visit a local charity or care establishment. The problem with creating situations like these is that they are often, for practical reasons, limited to small numbers. Situations can be set up within the classroom with the advantage of reaching greater numbers but realism may be lost.

■ Explore the idea of governors as link tutors for a year group or tutor group. This would not only bring them into more direct personal contact with pupils, but would also help provide the wider context and perspective from legal, social, business and economic institutions. With this link established, more opportunities for interchange can be identified. Some suggestions for further development of this role of link tutor could be:

> – *Involvement in the PSHE programmes,*
> *particularly focusing on those elements relating*
> *to citizenship. In this way the link governor*
> *becomes a source of information and a facilitator.*

– Working with members of the tutor group to produce an assembly with a citizenship theme to be put on before the whole year group.

– Working with the tutor group to help raise money for a local/national/ international charity. Matched funding arrangements could be negotiated here. If, for example, a school works with a local business or industry to raise funds for a local charity, then there is a pleasing result in that two distinct strands, education and business, come together to help a third in the wider community.

– Use of governors in appropriate lessons to encourage pupils to look at the wider perspective. This may develop into a series of lessons relating to the particular topic.

■ Liaison between a named governor and a specific department/area within the school. Attendance of that governor at department meetings when specific topics/issues are being discussed could bring about a 'citizenship' slant. Similarly, if whole or part of a training day was being used for department time on a particular topic, governors could contribute much.

Parents

Parents too have a huge contribution they can make in this area. The Home School Agreement, negotiated between parents, pupils and school, is in itself a classic example of citizenship in action, recognising as it does rights and responsibilities in all three parties forming the partnership.

In many ways, parents can be involved in citizenship activities in much the same way as governors. There is, however, one additional area of input parents may be able to make. This is in providing an insight into different cultural, religious and ethnic backgrounds. The calendar provides many opportunities for this, eg Chinese New Year (possibly through philosophy and belief, drama or art), Thanksgiving Day (possibly through history/English), Saints Days, Bastille Day (through modern languages), Passover and Diwali, etc. In practice this could range from bringing in costumes, artefacts and pictures to cooking a meal or re-enacting a situation.

CHAPTER 3

SOME GENERIC METHODS OF TEACHING CITIZENSHIP

In this chapter we give some thought to the use of a few generic techniques or methods that might be applied in any subject area. We believe that variety is the spice of life and the use of a wide variety of teaching and learning methods will help pupils with different preferred ways of learning and maintain the interest of all.

We propose to consider the following methods:

■ the use of drama and role play;

■ the use of work experience;

■ research and use of the Internet.

The use of drama and role play

A frequent argument about drama centres on whether it is a subject in its own right or a tool to deliver understanding within other subjects. Is its purpose the teaching of dramatic skills or should it bring about social understanding? Perhaps we can resolve this argument if we agree that there are two separate purposes. One of which, the development of dramatic skills to entertain, to move, to inform when actors perform to an audience is the prime outcome of drama lessons. Drama when used in a different environment has the second purpose. It is to provide an opportunity to experience a role rather than to give a polished representation of it. Within many school subjects, dramatic skills may be used but the person involved is not primarily an actor and gains from the experience an empathy or understanding of the feelings and emotions of the person whose role is being studied. Drama, then, is an aid to understanding as well as a way of employing a different teaching method to give variety and, hopefully, enjoyment alongside the learning.

Role play is a technique that can be used in almost every subject, but especially in PSHE, English and history. The value here is what pupils learn about being in a role. So, after appropriate research, a pupil could act out a scenario explaining what it was like to be a child worker in a textile factory in the early nineteenth century or explain why she, in the role of the suffragette Emily Wilding Davidson, decided to throw herself under the king's horse (if that is indeed what she did!). The pupil learns to identify and empathize with the character he or she is playing.

Role playing is a valuable technique for the teacher. It can provide participation, involvement and the opportunity for action learning. Participants act out (or practise) real life situations (or situations that could occur in real life) in a protected environment. Their behaviour, speech and feelings during the action form the basis for self-appraisal and feedback from others who have been observing. From this they will learn which behaviour, words and approaches are effective. They also have the opportunity to empathize with the character portrayed and to recognize a position that may be different from their own.

Role playing during lessons permits participants to experience the situation they play. They can learn what others see, hear and feel. Pupils can discover the impact their adopted attitudes and behaviour have and how they are perceived by others. This opportunity to look at life from another perspective is rare and useful.

Regardless of the precise situation, there are many common lessons to be learnt. These are most often in the understanding of difference and diversity. The ability to understand others' views, handle conflict, reach agreement or gain new awareness can also be improved through role playing. In addition, changes in attitude and perception are often the result of playing the role of someone else.

Choosing participants

When first introducing role play to a lesson there is bound to be a degree of uncertainty and apprehension among pupils unless they have previously been involved in role playing. For this reason it is often advisable to choose the most outgoing or confident pupils to have the first attempt (or, of course, someone who has done it before). It is sometimes a good idea to try and match people with their role-play characters but in many cases playing a character very different from oneself can become a real opportunity to explore others' attitudes and feelings. It is often not necessary, for instance, to find a girl to play a female part. However, to increase participants' comfort on their first attempt it may be advisable to choose roles that are not too distant from their own.

It is sometimes a valuable technique to use role reversal. For example, a pupil could usefully take the role of the teacher for a short spell and imagine the feelings of someone in that position.

Making the environment 'safe'

Any role play may induce anxiety, particularly for those who are unfamiliar with the process. There are several things that teachers can do to reduce anxiety levels:

- Make sure that everyone is absolutely clear about the aims of the session and what is expected.

- It must always be emphasized that the role play is an opportunity to learn. It is in no way intended to open anyone to ridicule or humiliation but rather to provide an opportunity from which to learn. There is no competition and no comparisons should be made.

- Everyone in the group must be made aware that they too will be participating. Try to create a co-operative, supportive atmosphere.

- Select role plays that are readily recognizable by the participants and start with simple cases that will produce successful outcomes.

- Allow the playing individuals to have a supporter or team with whom they confer before the role play, someone who is able to prompt if the player is losing the thread or is drying up.

- Reduce the exposure felt by the participants and allow the play to take place in groups of three, ie two players and an observer. The obvious disadvantage is the difficulty the teacher will have in keeping up with what is happening in several groups at once.

Review and feedback

On completion of the role play it is essential that players are able to reflect upon what has happened and to discuss what happened with the others.

CHECKLIST: CONDUCTING A ROLE PLAY

1. Explain the purpose of the session and of the role play in particular. Outline the skills that should be practised.

2. Select and reassure pupils and put them at ease with the idea of role playing.

3. Brief the players as appropriate and allow sufficient time for preparation.

4. Brief those not directly involved on what is required from them as observers. Give them the same briefing as the participants.

5. Encourage participants to get into role and improvise within the framework of the brief.

6. Check that everyone understands their role and their part in the exercise. Be prepared to answer questions and give clarification.

7. Start the role play and allow it to continue until a reasonable conclusion is reached, until the players dry up or there appears to be no further progress to be made or learning to be acquired. In the event of a breakdown it may be possible to pause, take stock and then continue. Alternatively get new pupils who are familiar with the roles to sit in and continue the action.

8. Review the process. Allow players the first say, followed by the observers. The teacher will need to control and direct the discussion to cover the main learning points.

9. The teacher should close with a summary of what worked well and what were the principal lessons.

Taking the 'hot seat'

This is a development of the basic role play idea. Whilst in character the pupil has to answer questions in a way that indicates how that person would have thought and acted. Pupils doing this need to understand the actions of the person they are interpreting and be able to argue in a way he or she would have done.

Some examples might be John Wilkes Booth defending his murder of Abraham Lincoln at the theatre or Pontius Pilate justifying his actions against Jesus Christ or a government minister explaining why he or she has had to take some course of action in a topical case or issue.

Conflict resolution

Drama has a huge role to play here. It can be used to help the resolution of an actual disagreement between two pupils, for example, and so can be an aid to pastoral/PSHE work. Each pupil involved could be asked to imagine what it might be like to be in the shoes of the other as a first step in understanding and reaching agreement or compromises. The same technique could be used within a philosophy and belief lesson to address and reach agreement about issues such as apartheid or religious or ethnic divides. Forum theatre is an example of this; pupils are encouraged to adopt a position and act out the views that a person in that position would hold.

Tableaux

In any situation where pupils work together their inter-personal skills and communication skills can be greatly enhanced and drama is one way of facilitating this. Tableaux, living sculpture or freeze frame is a technique that uses still images portrayed by individuals or a group. This can help pupils answer the question of how we look at people. Still images can capture different reactions, shades of emotion and body language. Group sculpts, in which an individual characterizes a group by arranging the people involved in such a way as to represent what they see as happening within the group, have a similar purpose.

Whole-group drama

Whole group drama, or group role plays, can be very useful in certain situations. Within PSHE, for example, a possible scenario is a newspaper editorial meeting to decide which articles are of the greater social importance and should, therefore, be included in the next edition. The articles could cover a whole range of situations. One pupil could be encouraged to play devil's advocate to promote deeper discussion.

A 'balloon' or 'lifeboat' debate

These debates, to decide who is to be thrown overboard to lighten the balloon, or eaten to allow the occupants of the lifeboat to survive, or who should be rescued in which order from a flooding cave are very powerful. The skills here are perhaps not so challenging dramatically, but characters involved need to empathize, sympathize and put forward reasoned arguments based on an understanding of a situation or of someone's worth to society.

Use of drama in other subjects

Within modern languages drama can be used to bolster confidence. The simple repetition of a phrase, useful for a certain situation and accompanied by appropriate gestures, can help pupils to feel more confident using a language which is not their own.

Within science, the presentation of experiments in a different way by, for example, public announcement/speaking, can be effective. Using pupils as electrons and demonstrating chemical bonding is another dramatic technique which helps learning.

Differentiation

As with any technique, some pupils will feel more confident with drama than others. Drama can be self-differentiating because of the skills, natural or learnt, of the pupil involved in the acting and these skills can be extended. One way to stretch skills could be to add extra complications to the scenario. These additions would be those complicating factors which occur in real life, eg a time pressure/deadline being introduced, the information that a specific piece of equipment which is badly needed has broken down, the sudden removal (or addition) of a key figure, etc.

The use of work experience

Through Key Stage 4 we should aim to prepare all pupils for the opportunities, responsibilities and experiences of adult life. Work experience not only provides an insight into particular occupations but also facilitates opportunities to learn, use and improve key skills. In today's workplace, employability requires individuals to have qualities and competencies to meet the changing needs of employers and customers. These start to be developed in effective work-experience programmes.

The notion of citizenship is not new. Many, if not all, of the aspects mentioned in the scheme of work which follows have or could be covered to some extent by work experience. It should be possible to cover many different aspects of the citizenship programme of study at Key Stage 4 by perhaps slightly amending and reviewing current practice. It must also be recognized that no two pupils will ever get the same learning from their particular placement nor will any one pupil learn all the aspects of citizenship from their experience.

A co-ordinated work experience scheme, that incorporates careful preparation and deliberate debrief as well as monitoring of placements, can provide a perfect opportunity for the individual to see and participate in citizenship. Pupils value the process even more when they are directly involved in making choices, in speaking to employers and in evaluating the experience once it is over.

> A substantial majority, four out of five pupils, is positive about work experience. The greatest influence of work experience is almost certainly upon their understanding of the everyday expectations made of an employee and their responsibilities in the workplace.
>
> Ofsted Annual Report 1998.

A well-planned and effective programme of work experience can enable pupils to develop an understanding of the work ethic, including the need for discipline at work, punctuality, employment contracts, the importance of health and safety, risk assessment and management, the hours of work required of employees in different jobs and the concept of conditions of service. It can also help pupils to gain a deeper appreciation of values and issues such as equality of opportunity in the workplace. The extent to which pupils

> benefit depends on the effectiveness of preparation and review by the school and the quality of the arrangements made by the employer.
>
> QCA/DfEE 1999(b).

The outline of the programme for work experience which follows is by no means intended as the benchmark by which all others should be measured. It is intended to provide an insight into what has worked in one place and initiate ideas of what might work for others. The stages discussed below show how the programme of study for citizenship might be covered by a work experience or careers-based activity.

Preparation

Pupils are asked to specify two areas of work they would like to experience as soon as they begin Year 10. This involves tutors and year team staff as well as parents and friends. Pupils are encouraged to discuss their options in order to choose a balanced – yet relevant – experience. Pupils research many occupations using the Internet. Some pupils liaise with employers with a view to arranging their own placement. This involves telephoning, completing letters of application and visiting the company. Some employers will interview pupils prior to offering work experience. All pupils need to contact employers about the general arrangements – for example, hours of work, lunchtime arrangements, dress – as well as confirming the nature of the work involved. Employers should be contacted by the school and asked to offer places that can be matched to pupils. A guide to work experience is sent to all employers. This outlines the expectations, both legally and from the school, for each placement. It also states what the employer can expect of the pupil and the school: from the pupil – contact prior to placement, the highest standards of behaviour and effort; from the school – details of pupils, including any relevant information (eg medical), a quick response to any queries and a teacher visit during the placement. Employers should also be given details of the work which will be set by school during work-experience and what implications this has for supervisors. Pupils, together with their employers, complete a work experience logbook (an excellent example has been developed collaboratively by Learning Partnership West, a consortium of regional education authorities – see 'Useful contacts' at the back of this book). The logbook provides the pupil with an opportunity to record achievements and experience and a chance for supervisors to indicate the quality of work and standards attained. The particular focus is likely to be on the key skills of numeracy, communication, working with others, use of information and communication ICT and problem-solving; all of these have a direct relevance to citizenship.

During the placement

Both pupils and employers have a contact number and name at school in case of any problem. Pupils receive a health and safety induction so they are fully aware of no-go areas, fire procedures and escape routes, etc. The member of staff due to visit makes contact by telephone to agree a convenient time. Ideally they will talk to both the employer and the pupil to check progress. This is an excellent time for pupils to be given the opportunity to discuss difficulties and problems and talk about their achievements as recorded in the logbook.

Debrief

Employers should be asked to sum up the placement in the logbook and to complete a short assessment sheet on the pupil. These provide excellent information for parents, staff and pupils when the time comes to discuss, review and evaluate the placement or work experience. Pupils should spend their first day back in school carrying out various activities to evaluate and consolidate their learning. Tutor group discussion and evaluation is useful and could incorporate:

- Group sessions which utilize the key skills of communication and problem solving.

- Drama workshops or role plays where incidents from placements are re-enacted and responded to in different ways. These provide an enjoyable yet powerful means of demonstrating how to manage and cope with many situations that can and do arise.

- Producing display work to show what the company does and how pupils' work fitted in.

- Letters of thanks are written, again providing an opportunity for reflection as well as more practice in the important skill of letter writing.

Pupils should complete evaluation forms where they are encouraged to highlight areas of success and failure of their placement. This information is vital if future programmes are to be improved. Parents and staff are asked to comment on the programme too.

LINKS WITH CITIZENSHIP

KNOWLEDGE AND UNDERSTANDING ABOUT BECOMING INFORMED CITIZENS

- All pupils are informed of both their rights and responsibilities during their work experience. Various exercises and activities convey these issues. Work in personal and social education, careers education and guidance literature and assemblies can all be used to draw out additional lessons.

- The need for mutual respect and understanding of the diverse regional, religious and ethnic identities in the UK are also stressed. For some pupils, work experience may provide their first glimpse of such diversity.

- The way business is done, the procedures and processes used are very important to employers. Pupils see these things in action not only on their placements but also in school prior to their departure with all the necessary paperwork and forms. For many young people, work experience is often their first real insight into how the economy functions. Work experience provides a powerful view of the role of business and financial services as well as the factors which affect them.

- Some pupils will experience voluntary work. This group should see how both groups and individuals can bring about social change locally, nationally, in Europe and internationally.

- Many pupils will see how the information available through the Internet is revolutionizing the way business is done. Others will learn how the media's role in society can affect opinion, through helping to design web sites, working for advertising agencies, newspapers and the radio.

- Many issues relating to the rights and responsibilities of consumers, employers and employees will be mentioned during work experience.

continued

continued

- The UK's relations in Europe can often come alive through work experience. Pupils see for the first time how our relations with our neighbours affect and produce opportunities for companies and employees.

- Wider issues such as global responsibility and sustainable development are factors for many companies. Large numbers of firms now have policies and procedures around environmental issues. Pupils are encouraged to seek them out and record them in their logbook.

DEVELOPING SKILLS OF ENQUIRY AND COMMUNICATION

- Pupils should be encouraged to research the company they will visit during work experience. In this way they will learn more about the nature of the employer by accessing information from different sources, eg the Internet and the press. They should be encouraged to scrutinize statistical and other information critically.

- Pupils should be asked to record significant events in detail whilst on placement. They will then be able to state their viewpoint and defend it. This can also be useful in the drama workshops and role plays on debrief day. An important part of a debrief day are the group and exploratory class discussion and debates.

DEVELOPING SKILLS OF PARTICIPATION AND RESPONSIBLE ACTION

- Throughout the work experience process pupils are expected to make decisions about their participation. They are required to help the process of finding a placement, they must respond to the work they are given to do responsibly. They are required to act as representatives of their school and to take part responsibly in the activities of their employer, respecting health and safety requirements, the norms of the host organization and helping the people in it, in some way, to do their work well.

- The period of evaluation on return to school should focus on the pupil's participation and should also require the individual to reflect on their participation in the work experience placement.

Research and use of the Internet

There are many sources of information available to teachers these days. Your school library, local libraries, county records office, city archives and museums of various types are readily accessible, and traditional text-based research techniques can yield excellent results. The information available can be in book, article or document form. However, it may be much quicker and easier to search for material on-line. Because of its speed, and the simplicity of access to huge amounts of information, the Internet is becoming an important source of information for all. With a good search engine, such as www.yahoo.com, www.lycos.com or www.altavista.com you can readily locate information on an enormous range of subjects. There are search engines of search engines; www.dogpile.com is one such, which simultaneously searches a large number of search engines for the cue you give it, and the resulting number of 'hits' on related web pages can be huge. The Internet is quick and easy to use; it is even fun. There is a huge amount of information and free resources available through computers.

A word of caution is appropriate here. The Internet has huge potential and enormous amounts of information but it has also the potential for pupils to stray into areas of undesirable subject matter, especially when carrying out unsupervised personal research on topics. It will be quite possible for strange

---

EXAMPLE: THE POWER OF THE INTERNET

When researching information for use in Chapter 7, to examine the ethics of recent scientific developments, we used www.webwombat.com as our search engine. We double clicked on 'Newspapers' and highlighted 'United Kingdom'. Back at the homepage, where the search facility is displayed, we then entered 'GM foods' and clicked on 'Search'. In seconds we were presented with a long list of data and the second item directed us to www.millennium-debate.org and this gave us a list (149 pages) of the latest articles published in a range of British newspapers with the headline and brief summary of the article. These covered both sides of the argument for and against GM food and were full of detailed information to inform the debate. Each article could be accessed in full from the screen and printed for use if required. The whole process took no more than ten minutes to access several useful articles and left us with a great sense of achievement.

and even unpalatable opinions to be expressed in school as a result of such activity and teachers will need to handle this when it arises. For further guidance on this issue you can refer to the document on Internet usage produced by the British Education and Communications Technology Agency (BECTA) and the DfEE www.vtc.ngfl.gov.uk/vtc/library/pub.html.

There are many uses of the Internet as far as citizenship is concerned; it is, after all, a global medium which can help people to become citizens of the world. Some useful Web sites are given below and reference is made to others throughout this book and its companion volume. One Web site for beginners, which has pages of hints, tips and references is www.etown.edu/vl. Go to this site and click on 'Starter Tips for Internet Research'. This US site also has huge numbers of other links to Web sites dealing with topical affairs.

■ Most government and local government offices/departments have Web sites. Many of these include useful statistics. The UK government information service can be found at http://open.gov.uk

■ Voluntary groups and charities have Web sites, eg www.oxfam.org.uk

■ National and local newspapers have Web sites, eg www.tes.co.uk for the *Times Educational Supplement*. These can be used to analyse the ways issues are reported and can help identify bias, even-handedness, etc. Editorials and readers' letters are also useful for this purpose.

■ BBC Online www.bbc.co.uk/education has linked access to a range of educational Web sites.

■ British Education and Communications Technology Agency, Virtual Teacher Centre Web site vtc.ngfl.gov.uk/vtc/library/pub.html is a huge resource for teachers on a wide range of subjects.

■ Citizen 21 www.citizen21.org.uk is an on-line resource for citizenship from which material can be downloaded. The Citizenship Foundation www.citfou.org.uk is a charity supporting citizenship education. The Council for Education in World Citizenship is an independent educational organization specializing in creating partnerships with local, national and global organizations to develop active learning opportunities in citizenship, www.cewc.org.uk

- Community Service Volunteers. This organization works with schools and colleges to enable young people to become active citizens through practical projects addressing community needs. www.csv.org.uk

- The main European Union Web site is at http://europa.eu.int and http://www.eun.org offers a civics section in its 'Virtual School' with a discussion forum and occasional contacts with MEPs.

- The Foreign and Commonwealth Office site www.fco.gov.uk has information on studying overseas cultures.

- Charter 88 is a campaign for a modern and fair democracy. Their site is at www.charter88.org.uk and they have a section on citizenship.

- The Hansard Society promotes knowledge about parliament and government. It can provide high quality material for mock elections in schools. www.hansardsociety.org.uk

- The Institute for Citizenship www.citizen.org.uk. The institute's aim is to promote citizenship by developing innovative projects for citizenship education.

- The National Curriculum Web site is at www.nc.uk.net

- www.NISS.ac.uk/world/schools.html provides a huge collated list of sources of information for schools.

- The Internet provides information concerning partner school opportunities (the international dimension). Some useful sites are:

    - *Environmental themes*   *www.life-link.org*

    - *The European Schoolnet*   *www.eun.org*

    - *Windows on the World*   *www.wotw.org.uk*

    - *On the line (Meridian Line)* *www.ontheline.org.uk*

- One World. www.oneworld.org is an organization dedicated to promoting human rights and sustainable development.

- The Public Record Office www.pro.gov.uk/education provide a number of resources for lessons, particularly in history, for Key Stages 3 and 4, some of which will be relevant for citizenship.

- Biz/ed is an excellent source of resource material for teaching business and economics http://bized.ac.uk/stafsup

- United Nations Association of the UK www.una-uk.org is a source of information about Model United Nations debates.

- World newspapers. www.webwombat.com provides details of how to contact over 10,000 worldwide newspapers for up-to-the-minute comment on events.

- On sites like www.FT.com you can register to receive e-mails on specified subjects so that you do not have to search – information arrives on the subject specified.

- There are sites that provide an answering service for questions. One such is www.ask.com a site from the Ask Jeeves organization.

- E-mail and the Internet can be used to gather views from other schools and groups throughout the world. The Internet provides 'chat' forums on specific subject areas (these are often cross referenced and readily discovered by search engine search strings) which, if properly supervised, provide the opportunity to talk in realtime to an expert or someone in another country about the subject of your interest.

- Government is promoting the idea of e-business or electronic commerce and an awareness of the technology and the information available is a major key skill required for jobs in the future. The intention is that each pupil at school should have access to the Internet by the year 2003.

- Video conferencing can be used to observe meetings and discussions of various groups or to conduct debates with people in other parts of the country or the world. There are examples where this has been set up between a school and a major engineering company for two-way links between design and technology students and a design engineer working on part design projects collaboratively.

- Pupils can set up school Web sites for interactive use.

- Opportunities could be sought for decision-making exercises and problem-solving activities between link schools. This could involve the use of video conferencing to generate debates.

Some examples of possible research work for pupils are given below.

EXAMPLE: THE EUROPEAN UNION

Pupils are asked to prepare an information pack on the EU, which could be word-processed or desk-top published, on the theme 'How does the EU affect our lives?'

Pupils will first need to identify which are the member states of the EU. A blank map of Europe divided into countries without names would assist this process.

- www.europa.eu.int is the European Commission Web site and contains a wealth of information. The abc of the European Union www.europa.eu.int/abc-en.htm gives a background to the EU.

- www.europa.eu.int/comm/dg03 is the Web site for the EU Internal Market.

- www.europa.eu.int/comm/dg1a/enlarge/ is the Web site for EU Foreign Affairs and Enlargement.

- EU Customs and Taxation can be found on www.europa.eu.int/comm/dg21

- The EU database for documents and legislation is on www.europa.eu.int/scadplus

- EU publications can be sought via the London Office of the European Commission on www.cec.org.uk/pubs

- The Department of Trade and Industry and its links with Europe can be found at www.dti.gov.uk/europe

- The Confederation of British Industry can be found at www.cbi.org.uk

---

EXAMPLE: RUBBISH AND RECYCLING

This is a highly topical issue and there is a lot of information in the media on recycling, landfill, burning etc. This exercise compares the most recent information with OECD data on waste disposal from 1990 (Table 3.1). Use an Internet search engine such as www.yahoo.com, www.lycos.com or www.altavista.com to find the OECD Web site and search for the most recent version of the chart. Using the most recent data obtained, answer these questions:

■ What percentage of total waste is recycled in the UK?

■ How does this compare with other countries?

■ In which countries are landfill sites most important as a means of disposal?

■ Which countries incinerate the highest percentage of their rubbish?

■ What are the most significant changes in the period between the two sets of data?

Search for additional data on the Internet. Suggest pressure groups as a good starting point, eg Greenpeace www.greenpeace.org or Friends of the Earth www.foe.co.uk. Other good sites would be daily papers eg, www.the-times.co.uk, www.dailytelegraph.co.uk, www.mirror-group.co.uk, www.dailyexpress.co.uk, www.associatednewspapers.co.uk, www.guardian.co.uk and also government Web sites.

Table 3.1 Disposal of municipal waste 1990 ('000 tonnes)

Country	Total collected	Composting	Incineration	Landfill	Recycle	Other
USA	177,500	3,800	28,900	118,300	26,500	–
Japan	49,271	4	36,676	16,809	1,684	–
Denmark	2,430	230	1,320	720	160	–
Finland	3,100	50	50	2,400	600	–
West Germany	21,172	805	4,742	14,842	–	783
Ireland	1,100	–	–	1,100	–	–
Italy	20,033	–	1,262	17,990	–	781
Netherlands	7,430	295	2,490	3,197	300	15
Spain	12,546	2,564	606	9,376	–	–
Sweden	3,200	100	1,300	1,400	400	–
UK	20,000	–	2,500	14,000	–	1,000

'–' = figures are unavailable. Note: definitions may vary from country to country, hence the total collected may differ from the sum of the other figures in the row.

Source: OECD, *Environmental Data Compendium*, 1993.

EXAMPLE: COVERAGE OF A NEWS STORY IN THE PRESS

Take any news story gaining widespread coverage and compare the treatment by different news-papers using content analysis. Look at the amount of coverage, which pages (ie front page, inside feature) headlines and pictures, opinion columns, the attitude of the paper. (The teacher would need to give some background on the press, eg tabloids, broadsheets and their political affiliation.)

A selection of web sites: www.the-times.co.uk, www.dailytelegraph.co.uk, www.mirror-group.co.uk, www.dailyexpress.co.uk, www.guardian.co.uk, www.associatednewspapers.co.uk. This could be extended to cover television news if wished, as TV has a duty of impartiality.

LINKS WITH CITIZENSHIP

KNOWLEDGE AND UNDERSTANDING ABOUT BECOMING INFORMED CITIZENS

- The Internet can provide an enormous amount of information about citizenship. Government, media, voluntary organizations, EU, UN and other international Web sites (many listed above) are very rich sources of high quality knowledge and information. Material on topics including government and democracy, the economy, environmental issues, the role of the media and international relations are there for the taking.

- The web can be used by the teacher to prepare information and statistics for lessons or by pupils to do their own research and form their own opinions on the topics they research.

DEVELOPING SKILLS OF ENQUIRY AND COMMUNICATION

- The very use of the Internet facilitates the acquisition of skills of enquiry. The computer is essentially the ultimate communication medium.

- Care must be taken, however, not to neglect the other sources of information in libraries and printed information and from first-hand research on the ground.

DEVELOPING SKILLS OF PARTICIPATION AND RESPONSIBLE ACTION

Usually, searching the Internet will be an essentially lone pastime. However, if pupils can contribute to forum debates and (carefully selected and screened) chat rooms there are opportunities to participate in wider debate in the community outside the school.

PART 2

TEACHING CITIZENSHIP IN SUBJECT LESSONS

The activities in this book, and its companion volume, are ones that give ideas and pointers as well as providing specific material. They are not intended to be prescriptive. They may be lifted directly from the page and put into practice in the classroom. They may be used as templates for a wide range of similar activities which individual schools and teachers can create to meet their own teaching and learning goals more closely. If, as we hope, the material appeals to teachers it will be useful both as a dip-in resource and as a prompt, or thought starter, for more different activities and lessons.

In all the activities described in this book there is an implicit requirement for the teacher to ensure that lessons for citizenship are made clear. In the course of discussions, as a response to questions or as part of the normal delivery of the lesson, there will be many and various opportunities to clarify an issue or make a point that will extend the pupils' knowledge of citizenship. These opportunities should be grasped as they appear, whether or not the lesson has as one of its aims some part of the citizenship curriculum. However, where the lesson does have such an aim, it becomes even more important to seize the opportunity to provide additional clarification or learning whenever possible.

Not every subject will readily address all the aspects of citizenship contained in the curriculum but almost every subject will be able to raise issues of citizenship from time to time, either as a conscious intention or because the opportunity arises. Just as a good parent will seize the opportunity to push home a lesson about safety or honesty when it arises, so teachers should be alert to the opportunity to draw lessons for citizenship.

It will never be possible, in a book like this, to foresee each and every one of the learning outcomes that may emerge from a lesson and we anticipate that there will be many more beneficial outcomes than those that we have specifically listed under each activity. Equally, depending on the nature and direction of some of the discussion, it may not always prove possible to extract all of those that we have listed.

The material in this book was provided by a large number of people and inevitably appears with some differences in format and structure but we believe that we have maintained a consistent standard for that material.

CHAPTER 4

CITIZENSHIP IN THE PSHE LESSON

Inherent in the teaching of Personal Social and Health Education (PSHE) is the issue of values. The whole area could easily be one of controversy. Whose values should be taught? Should values be imposed anyway? Many of these issues leave teachers profoundly uncomfortable, particularly when the subjects under discussion impinge on what is essentially political. The arguments over Clause 28 of the Local Government Act and how the issue of homosexuality should be addressed are sufficient to illustrate how sensitive an area the teaching of values can be.

In this chapter we have suggested a range of activities that are designed to raise awareness of government, of public institutions and of democratic processes. The approach does not presuppose any particular stance or political slant. The activities described are intended to raise the quality of rational debate, awareness of democratic processes and of local community issues.

The activities are as follows:

- Key Stage 3

    - *A single lesson 'Government and its workings'.*

    - *Five or six lessons 'Improving the local community'.*

- Key Stage 4

    - *A series of up to six lessons and activities 'The functions of government'.*

    - *A series of up to five lessons of 'Mock elections'.*

PSHE/citizenship, Key Stage 3
TITLE: Government and its workings

TIME REQUIRED: Single lesson plus preparation

AIMS AND OBJECTIVES

- To give pupils an awareness and understanding of the functions of government.

- To show that there are different levels of government.

- To demonstrate the main functions/responsibilities of these different levels.

- To stress the importance of voting.

Introduction

Brainstorm to get from pupils their understanding (or otherwise!) of the different levels of government and their function.

Discussion

For this four sets of cards are needed. These cards should have written on them the following:

- Different levels of government – town/parish, district/unitary authority, county, national, European.

- Names, eg Keynsham, Bath and North East Somerset, etc. (This will need to be specific to the area of the school.)

- Meeting places, eg town hall, Westminster, etc.

- Responsibilities, eg lighting, building development and planning, education, defence, equal opportunities, etc.

Groups/pairs match up the cards. Some responsibilities may fall into more than one level. Blank cards can be available for pupils to add their own ideas.

Groups report back and share ideas. 'Correct' answers are given (a further 5 minutes).

Development

Why is it important to understand how the levels of government work?

- Generate a discussion using a comparison with school systems based on the idea of 'knowing whom to approach for what' and so reinforcing the understanding that different levels have different responsibilities.

- Get pupils individually to say why they would use particular points of contact, local or national, to gain information or resolve problems and so stress the importance of needing to use them, ie by voting at appropriate times.

Implications/conclusion

Pupils to choose *one* election and say why they would vote in it. Prompts could be given for this, eg accessibility of candidates, how an individual's life will be affected (long/short term), ideas on perceived power of the organization being elected, etc.

LINKS WITH CITIZENSHIP

KNOWLEDGE AND UNDERSTANDING ABOUT BECOMING INFORMED CITIZENS

- Pupils learn about central and local government, the public services they offer and how they are financed.

- They learn about the key characteristics of parliamentary and other forms of government.

continued overleaf

continued

- They learn about the electoral process and the importance of voting.

DEVELOPING SKILLS OF ENQUIRY AND COMMUNICATION

- Pupils learn to think about topical political and social issues and form and justify a personal opinion about such issues.

- They contribute to group and exploratory class discussions and take part in debates.

PSHE/citizenship, Key Stage 3
TITLE: Improving the local community

TIME REQUIRED: Five or six lessons plus preparation

AIMS AND OBJECTIVES

- To encourage pupils to explore their local community area.

- To identify an area of the local community which needs to be improved in some way.

- To allow pupils the opportunity to research local views on the needs in the area through a survey of residents.

- To show pupils how to make simple designs and planning drawings to show intended improvements.

- To enable pupils to have a knowledge of the financial and legal aspects of planning and to make contact with relevant housing and planning departments to find out how regulations/local bylaws will affect any improvements planned.

- To cost the improvements and to investigate ways of paying for them, including the possibility of sponsorship from local businesses.

■ To evaluate the success of the proposals with local residents.

Introduction

Pupils should be asked to spend time in lesson, or as a task set over a weekend or holiday, to explore their local area and to identify areas needing to be improved. This may be a park, a play area, a patch of wasteland or land bordering a river or other natural feature. Pupils can then discuss the areas identified and collectively choose one that provides them with the greatest opportunity to make their suggested improvements within the time allocated.

Discussion

Pupils should brainstorm all the different aspects of their task, ie planning, finance, information gathering, production of drawings/models. Groups of pupils should take responsibility for each of these areas and investigate how to obtain the necessary information.

Development

Over a number of lessons pupils should be involved in writing and completing questionnaires and circulating them to local residents in the area affected, costing items required for the work, speaking to council officials and local businesses. Drawings or models will need to be made. Analysis of the questionnaire responses from local residents will need to be done and the views of planning and amenity officers from the local council will need to be obtained before detailed drawings and financial costs can be finalized.

Implementation

When drawings and costings have been finalized pupils should invite local residents and councillors in to school to look at their proposals and discuss their viability. The local press may also be interested in their work. Assuming there are no objections, work then starts. Some may be done by pupils, some may have to be contracted. The planning and supervision of the work will be a major challenge for pupils.

LINKS WITH CITIZENSHIP

KNOWLEDGE AND UNDERSTANDING ABOUT BECOMING INFORMED CITIZENS

- Pupils learn from studying central and local government, the public services they offer and how they are financed as well as the regulations governing development work.

- They study the work of community-based groups.

- They recognize the importance of meeting needs of different people fairly.

DEVELOPING SKILLS OF ENQUIRY

- Pupils learn from thinking about topical political, social and cultural issues.

- They express and justify a personal opinion about such issues orally and in writing.

- They contribute to group and exploratory class discussions.

DEVELOPING SKILLS OF PARTICIPATION AND RESPONSIBLE ACTION

- Pupils learn from using their imagination to consider other people's experiences and being able to think about, express and explain views that are not their own.

- They participate responsibly in group and community activities and contribute to the welfare of the wider community.

PSHE/citizenship, Key Stage 4
TITLE: The functions of government

TIME REQUIRED: Up to six lessons plus preparation beginning two to three months ahead

AIMS AND OBJECTIVES

- To give pupils an awareness and understanding of the functions of government.

- To develop pupils' awareness and understanding of the role of democratic institutions and justice systems in Britain and Europe.

- To give them the opportunity to meet real-life councillors, etc and to question them on their role and responsibility.

- To increase their awareness of local and national issues and the choices/complexities of government.

- To develop pupils' skills of enquiry and communication by working in various sized groups to hold exploratory discussions and formal debates.

- To ensure that pupils are introduced to a wide variety of political views.

Planning and preparation

At least two months before the proposed course, write to potential speakers inviting them to take part in the course and asking them to confirm dates. It is important to do this early as many of these people's diaries get very full. You may wish to ensure that all the main political parties are represented and that, where possible, a balance between male and female speakers is achieved.

When you hear from the speakers, you should use the opportunity to check whether speakers would like to see the pupils' questions in advance. You should also find out whether they are expecting to run workshops/discussion groups or plan just to give a talk followed by a question and answer session. This may affect your room and equipment bookings.

When dates and details have been confirmed, select and book appropriate rooms and equipment. Do any speakers require projectors, etc? Speak to the care-taker/year head to sort out room layouts (chairs, etc) for venues. Confirm bookings IN WRITING.

Two or three weeks before proposed course

Prepare and photocopy lesson plans and resources for colleagues taking lessons. Circulate timetable for lessons to colleagues so pupils and teachers know what to expect week by week. This should be displayed in the tutor room. Negotiate with the head teacher/senior management team/year head how the guests will be received and greeted.

One week before

Using different tutor times, ask pupils to come up with questions for the different speakers (within group and whole-class discussions). You should use topics in the news to encourage pupils to think about broad issues. Some speakers would appreciate knowing the issues that have been discussed before they arrive (check, see above).

You could have a rolling programme of discussion for each forthcoming speaker. If there is a class which has to miss seeing the MP or another key speaker, you could ask them to write questions to be passed to other classes and raised with the MP so they feel involved. This will help maintain the momentum of the course between the weekly lessons.

Prepare a stand-by lesson (perhaps using some of the extension material below) in case a speaker lets you down at the last minute.

Before each lesson

Set up equipment for each session (projectors, etc) and check/organize chairs. Check that each teacher is clear what is expected/where the pupils need to be. Make sure each guest is to be greeted and offered coffee, etc before PSHE. Organize two pupils to be sent to meet and greet the guest and escort them to the room for their talk.

Table 4.1 Suggested programme for functions of government course

Week	Group A	Group B	Group C
Week 1 (optional but advised)	Introduction – Importance of political education and who has power/influence over you? (See below.)		
Week 2	Local councillor (name) Room? Equipment? Met by….?	Magistrate (name) Room? Equipment? Met by….?	MEP/European Contact (name) Room? Equipment? Met by….?
Week 3	MEP/European Contact (name) Room? Equipment? Met by….?	Local councillor (name) Room? Equipment? Met by….?	Magistrate (name) Room? Equipment? Met by….?
Week 4	Magistrate (name) Room? Equipment? Met by….? (may decide MP should see whole year)	MP (name) Room? Equipment? Met by….? (may decide Head should meet and greet)	
Week 5	Suggested follow up work: Circulation of information/word search/create your own political party		

The course

Week 1: Introduction – the importance of political education

In these lessons there are times when small groups are suggested as a forum for discussion. These could be varied by ability/sex/friendship etc to offer the widest possible opportunity for pupils to develop their communication skills. You may choose to select one or two of the group activities to focus on in detail.

Ask pupils to write down in the back of their PSHE books as many of the school rules as they can remember.

Organize pupils into small groups. They should:

- decide how they are going to share the school rules as a group;

- try to reduce all the rules to one sentence that they can all agree on;

- report back to the class, each group giving their single-sentence rules.

Tutor to explain that they have been behaving as political animals. On board, write: *Polis* = 'city', *Polites* = 'citizenship' in Ancient Greek.

Whenever people live/work together, there are politics. How people get on, and the rules they follow when working together, are interesting. Ask pupils if they can suggest any 'rules' governing their behaviour in the small groups. Write these on the board.

Give pupils a list of people in schools and ask them to rank them according to their *influence* and *power* in school. Conduct a brief class discussion about the difference between power and influence (see Table 4.2). Again, groups will need to nominate a spokesperson, perhaps someone different. When they feed back to the class, they should be ready to explain their reasons.

- Pupils should work in small groups. Each group will need to select a spokesperson.

- Ask them to consider the rules on the board about how they work with each other (later ask them if they can suggest more rules).

Table 4.2 Who holds power/influence in school?

Year 7 pupil	Head of house	Year head	Tutor
Librarian	Geography teacher	A good student	Head Teacher
School caretaker	A badly-behaved student	School governor	Department head
Year 13 pupil	English teacher	Science technician	PE teacher

Table 4.3 Who holds power/influence in Britain today?

Government	Trades unions	Parents
Employers	Members of Parliament	Newspapers/magazines
Local councils	European Union	Religious groups
Judges	Pop stars	Police
Multinational businesses	Teachers	Footballers

■ The spokesperson should present back to the whole class. Ask the pupils in small groups to arrange members of society in rank order of influence and/or power over them and/or over an adult and/or over society. Each small group could look at the same one comparing their results or you could assign different rankings to different groups and ask them to feed back to the whole class (see Table 4.3).

Weeks 2 to 4: visiting speakers

- If you are circulating the information as a follow-up activity, you should encourage pupils to note down key points during the discussion with particular speakers. This may be an effective means of encouraging active participation (see below).

- Send commendations to pupils who have worked well during sessions. This will encourage others the following week.

- Remember to send letters thanking the visiting speakers. If appropriate, ask the head teacher/head of year to sign.

Week 5 and beyond: possible extension activities

Circulation of information

Some pupils may not have had the opportunity to hear a particular talk. You could ask groups who did to prepare an A4 sheet summarizing key points to circulate to other tutor groups. This will depend on how you split the year group for the talks. The pupils will need to negotiate to decide the key points from the relevant talks and will then need to decide how best to present the information in a helpful and interesting manner.

Word Search

Generate a Word Search on the subject of local, national and European politics for pupils to complete and include a definition of all of the terms you have used to increase pupils' understanding. This may be a useful 'filler' where there are last-minute cancellations from speakers. It can also be used as a useful means of broadening the pupils' understanding before creating their own political party. See Table 4.4 for possible ideas and definitions.

Invent your own political party!

Pupils have now had the opportunity to view local and national policies of the day through the eyes of experienced politicians. It is now their turn! If they were critical of what they saw, how would they suggest things could be improved in Britain?

How far you take this and how many of the following you choose to develop will obviously depend on the time available. Pupils could be organized in friendship, mixed sex or ability groups.

Table 4.4 Word Search definitions

Cabinet	The team of MPs chosen by the Prime Minister to run the main government areas.
Candidate	A person putting him- or herself up for election as a councillor or MP. They will normally represent a particular party.
Civil Service	People employed to carry out the wishes of government.
Constituency	The fixed area of voters who elect a representative at local, national or European level.
Council	An elected body who discuss and make decisions that affect a local area (eg Bristol).
Democracy	A system of government where the people (ie everyone over 18 years old) elect the leaders.
Downing Street	The residence of the Prime Minister and Chancellor of the Exchequer.
Election	An opportunity for people to vote on a particular date.
European Parliament	Every member state of the EU elects MEPs who handle European issues.
European Union	European countries which have formed a Union to work with each other.
General Election	The process by which the whole country votes for a new House of Commons.
Government	The body of people ruling the country. (In Britain, this is normally one political party.)
House of Commons	The main chamber of parliament – the 'Lower House' where MPs debate.
House of Lords	The 'Upper House' of Parliament where Lords and Bishops sit.
Laws	Rules and regulations decreed by Parliament that affect our lives.

continued overleaf

Table 4.4 continued

Lobby	To try to persuade an MP to act in your interest or on your behalf. (From the lobbies, or antechambers of the House of Commons).
Magistrate	An unpaid (usually) judge who deals with 97% of criminal cases in Britain, some civil cases and passes on the rest of cases to the Crown Court.
Manifesto	The plans of a political party that they promise to introduce if elected.
MEP	Member of the European Parliament – represents us in Strasbourg.
Minister	A member of a government with responsibility for a particular job (for example the Minister of Defence).
Official Opposition	Usually the party with the second biggest number of MPs in the House of Commons. They are there to check all views are discussed.
Parliament	This term includes the monarchy and the Houses of Commons and Lords.
Political Party	People who share similar beliefs become members. There can be differences of opinion within one party.
Queen or King	The Head of State.
Speaker	The chairperson of debates in the House of Commons.
United Nations (UN)	A form of world council where international discussions can take place. Britain is a permanent member of the Security Council, the most powerful body within the UN.
Voting	Choosing a representative in an election or expressing support for an idea.

■ Select at least three key issues, eg environment, education, health, foreign policy, housing, crime (violence, drugs, etc). Within the groups, ask pupils to discuss and negotiate 'policies'.

■ How would they improve on the current situation?

■ Where would the money come from?

■ Ask them to prepare a speech for a class debate. This could be followed up by a class 'election'.

■ Ask them to develop a campaign: name/poster/slogans, etc. In addition, ask them to write a commentary to suggest at whom these are aimed.

Conclusions/implications

This set of activities would be an excellent precursor to a mock election at the school, see the next activity in this chapter. There is further information on this issue in the sister volume by the same authors, *Developing Citizenship in Secondary Schools*, Chapter 4.

LINKS WITH CITIZENSHIP

KNOWLEDGE AND UNDERSTANDING ABOUT BECOMING INFORMED CITIZENS

■ Pupils learn about the work of Parliament, government and the courts in making and shaping the law.

■ They learn about the importance of playing an active part in democratic and electoral processes.

■ They learn about the United Kingdom's relations in Europe, including the European Union.

continued overleaf

continued

DEVELOPING SKILLS OF ENQUIRY AND COMMUNICATION

- Pupils learn to think about topical political, moral, social or cultural issues, problems or events in creating their own party policies and by listening to guest speakers.

- They express, justify and defend orally and in writing their personal opinions about such issues.

- They contribute to group and exploratory class discussions, and take part in formal debates.

DEVELOPING SKILLS OF PARTICIPATION AND RESPONSIBLE ACTION

- Pupils learn to take part responsibly in school and group activities contributing their own skills in the most appropriate way.

PSHE/citizenship, Key Stage 4
TITLE: Mock elections

TIME REQUIRED: Four or five lessons plus preparation

AIMS AND OBJECTIVES

- To enable pupils to find out about local and national government.

- To identify an issue which is important to the pupils.

- To nominate candidates willing to take a range of different views of the chosen issue.

- To enable pupils to present a reasoned point of view both visually and orally.

- To produce written and visual material to support the views of each candidate.

- To allow pupils to campaign, carrying out canvassing and polling to select a winning candidate.

- To contact existing councillors/local MP to discuss the election process.

- To evaluate the success of the campaigns.

Introduction

Pupils brainstorm school or national issues to identify one that is considered important to them and then research more about the issues (including use of the Internet). Pupils can talk to local government members to establish the correct procedure for running an election and then set up systems for the nomination of candidates.

Discussion

Once candidates have been identified manifestos can be produced, posters circulated and canvassing carried out. Publicity surrounding the events of polling day can be set in place and assemblies can be used to provide information and encourage participation by all pupils.

Development

Polling day will take place and counting of the votes and publication of results will follow. Candidates should make speeches thanking their voters and campaign teams. A member of the winning party could be invited to address pupils on why they thought their campaign was particularly successful.

Implications/conclusion

Pupils can evaluate the success of their campaigns by looking at voting figures and asking others how aware they were of each of the candidates and their campaign issues.

LINKS WITH CITIZENSHIP

KNOWLEDGE AND UNDERSTANDING ABOUT BECOMING INFORMED CITIZENS

- Pupils learn to understand the work of Parliament, government and the courts in making and shaping law.

- They recognize the importance of playing an active part in democratic and electoral processes.

- They identify the opportunities that exist for individuals and voluntary groups to bring about social change locally, nationally, in Europe and internationally.

DEVELOPING SKILLS OF ENQUIRY

- Pupils learn to research topical political, spiritual, moral, social or cultural issues using information from different sources, including ICT-based sources. They gain an awareness of the use and abuse of statistics. All this comes from the creation of their own political manifestos and election publicity.

- They express, justify and defend orally and in writing a personal opinion about issues or events as part of their campaigning.

- They contribute to group and exploratory class discussions and take part in formal debates with other candidates and with supporters and opponents.

DEVELOPING SKILLS OF PARTICIPATION AND RESPONSIBLE ACTION

- Pupils learn to use their imagination to consider other people's experiences. They must think about how to meet the needs and expectations of others and how to communicate with them.

- They negotiate, decide and take part responsibly in school activities and, by inference, in community or public life.

- They reflect on the process of participating through a formal evaluation of the success (or otherwise) of campaigns.

CHAPTER 5

ENGLISH

English provides a very powerful medium for the teaching of values and citizenship. It can introduce the current and historical social, moral, cultural and political values of the country through a study of its literature. Issues of democracy, conflict, diversity, law and fairness, rights and responsibilities, etc can be addressed simply and directly through many works and through discussions about the values and beliefs that underlie or are represented in the narrative.

Through the study of literature it is also eminently possible to explore the differences in culture, mores and attitudes and beliefs of people different from ourselves.

This process can directly affect pupils' views of the world. Guiding the development of that view, among the many and varied world views available in literature, is the challenge for the English teacher. What values, if any, are to be taught? Or are different values to be explored and discussed so that pupils can form their own views? Guiding pupils through the complexities, diversity, paradoxes, harsh realities and ambiguities of life as depicted in literature or the media is a key role of the English teacher.

In this chapter we have included the following activities:

- Key Stage 3

    - *Two lessons examining the effect of advertising using the concept of an environmentally friendly toy.*

    - *A single lesson using* The Ballad of Reading Gaol *to examine poetry as a force for change.*

    - *A single lesson using poetry to explore power and oppression.*

■ Key Stage 4

    – *A double lesson using* Examination Day *to expose the need to think for yourself at GCSE level.*

    – *A short series of lessons exploring the media and its influence and linking that to opinion forming and expression of those opinions.*

English/citizenship, Key Stage 3
TITLE: The effect of advertising

TIME REQUIRED: Two lessons/one double lesson plus preparation

AIMS AND OBJECTIVES

For citizenship:

■ To recognize the importance of media in society.

■ To recognize that pupils are consumers and to encourage them to become more discerning ones.

■ To raise awareness of environmental issues and to make pupils consider how these should be introduced to children of different ages.

For English:

■ To develop pupils' reading and writing skills with increased understanding of task, audience and purpose and the importance of presentation.

■ To develop pupils' speaking and listening skills with opportunities to contribute to group and class discussions, using their imagination and negotiating within a small team.

Introduction

This lesson takes the form of discussions about advertising and its effect followed by practical work and discussion around the design and advertising of an environmentally friendly toy.

Discussion

Examine some adverts for toys. Discuss with pupils what the advertising is doing. How does it seek to influence you to buy? Get small groups to discuss the pressures that advertising can generate, eg peer pressure, pressure on poor parents, fashion and 'everyone has one' ideas etc.

Brainstorm what is meant by 'environmentally friendly'. How might that be translated into the design and production of a toy?

Development

Ask pupils individually to come up with an idea for an environmentally friendly toy or game and then in small groups negotiate and decide which idea to work on further.

Groups need to consider their target market or audience and the teacher could give them specific age ranges to focus their ideas. The pupils should be encouraged to divide tasks among themselves and to negotiate. If possible provide a real audience for their work (eg head of year, tutor, department head); the pupils would then be able to make a presentation of the product, their advertising and how they will launch their product.

Take care to ensure that the emphasis is correctly placed on the messages and positioning of the adverts rather than on producing high-quality design and artwork.

Implications/conclusion

This lesson will develop skills of close reading and an understanding of the purpose of advertising. Pupils will experience the way different messages are targeted. They should begin to become more discerning in their reading or acceptance of advertisements in the future.

LINKS WITH CITIZENSHIP

KNOWLEDGE AND UNDERSTANDING ABOUT BECOMING INFORMED CITIZENS

- Pupils learn to understand the role of the media in society.

DEVELOPING SKILLS OF ENQUIRY AND COMMUNICATION

- Pupils learn to think about social and environmental issues.
- They express and justify their opinions on these issues.
- They contribute to class discussions.

DEVELOPING SKILLS OF PARTICIPATION AND RESPONSIBLE ACTION

- Pupils learn to negotiate and decide – from the process of agreeing which idea to progress.
- They take part responsibly in group activities.

English/citizenship, Key Stage 3
TITLE: 'The Ballad of Reading Gaol' by Oscar Wilde

TIME REQUIRED: A single lesson plus preparation

AIMS AND OBJECTIVES

For citizenship:

- To consider jail as punishment and to recognize that the justice system is not static but changing and developing.

For English:

- To introduce Oscar Wilde as a writer and to consider the context of the poem, and poetry as a force for social change. Pupils will also learn about the rhyme sequence and structure of poetry.

- To allow pupils to approach a pre-twentieth century text.

- To increase their confidence in reading and understanding such work.

Background

The pre-twentieth century poetry unit scheme of work will involve the close reading of a pre-twentieth century narrative poem. This could include the analysis of the language of a small section (including a detailed look at similes and metaphors), dramatic presentation of several verses in groups and/or a creative piece (perhaps a letter to the family from jail in this example).

Introduction

Do not mention the title. Choose several verses to read to the pupils asking them to guess where they think poem is set.

Discussion

Conduct a whole-class discussion to establish where the poem is set, then ask why jail? Draw out punishment/deterrent/revenge/re-education, etc. Brainstorm – do they think it is successful? Why? Conduct a class discussion giving reasons. Why was Oscar Wilde jailed? Suggestions/possibilities before telling them he was jailed for homosexuality. Discuss the rights and wrongs of his imprisonment and consider how social views/values have changed.

Hand out small sections of the poem to (mixed ability) groups. Ask them to find and list information about the conditions in jail at that time. They should try to consider how it might differ from today. Conduct a class discussion around the reasons for and against treating prisoners humanely. Consider issues of social responsibility.

Implications/conclusion

Consider people's rights and responsibilities to the community and whether or not punishment fits the crime.

Consider the legal and human rights involved in this example and explore how the criminal justice system functions in this area.

Raise and discuss a related current political or social issue.

LINKS WITH CITIZENSHIP

KNOWLEDGE AND UNDERSTANDING ABOUT BECOMING INFORMED CITIZENS

- Pupils learn about legal and human rights and how they relate to citizens, including the way the criminal and civil justice systems operate.

- They learn about the importance of a free press, and the media's role in society in providing information and affecting opinion.

DEVELOPING SKILLS OF ENQUIRY AND COMMUNICATION

- Pupils learn to examine topical political, social and cultural issues from different perspectives.

- They express, justify and defend their personal opinions about the issues.

- They contribute to group and exploratory class discussions.

DEVELOPING SKILLS OF PARTICIPATION AND RESPONSIBLE ACTION

- Pupils learn to use their imagination to consider other people's experiences and be able to think about, express, explain and critically evaluate views that are expressed in the ballad or in discussion.

- They take part responsibly in group activities.

English/citizenship, Key Stage 3
TITLE: Power and oppression

TIME REQUIRED: A single lesson plus preparation

RESOURCES REQUIRED

A range of material around the subject of power and oppression. Examples include:

Telephone Conversation, Wole Soyinka (from *The Poetry of Protest*, 1991, edited by S. Fuller).

Back in the Playground Blues, Adrian Mitchell (from *Squeeze Words Hard*, 1990, A. Ebborn and M. Alcorn).

Not in India, Sadi Hussain (from *The Poetry of Protest*).

Don't Interrupt!, Demetroulla Vassili (from *Squeeze Words Hard*).

Presents from My Aunts in Pakistan, Half-Caste (from *NEAB Anthology*, 1996).

AIMS AND OBJECTIVES

For citizenship:

- To consider who has influence over our lives beyond our parents and teachers.

- To recognize that abuses can take place.

- To recognize stereotyping and different forms of prejudice (sexism, racism, homophobia, ageism, etc).

- To increase political awareness.

- To analyse one poem on a topic accessible to all pupils (eg bullying, parent/guardian versus a child) to highlight how language and form help to get the message across.

For English:

- To raise the question 'Why poetry?'

- To establish what poetry and literature can bring to issues of this sort.

- To recognize the value of poetry.

Background

The poetry unit scheme of work will include reading and listening to a wide range of poetry in different forms from a variety of cultures, addressing different issues of power relationships. Pupils are asked to compare, discuss and respond to poetry, including the written form, and to prepare a group dramatic presentation of a given poem. They are asked to write their own poem and short creative responses. If there is time, they will prepare a collage to include their work plus newspaper cuttings and appropriate song lyrics of their choice.

Introduction

Whole-class discussion 'Who has power over you?' Brainstorm, using the board: use questions to draw out issues of government and the wider community and examples of where things go wrong. Use current affairs/stories to try to draw out current government issues. Try to get pupils to address the idea of 'stereotyping' (eg take pupils with blonde hair and make abusive 'blondist' remarks about them). Ask what you are doing. Ask for specific examples of stereotyping (eg sexism, racism, homophobia, ageism, etc).

Development

Ask the question 'Why poetry?' Why not an advert saying 'Racism is bad!'? Draw out the very personal nature of poetry that allows readers to draw their own conclusions.

Hand out a copy of a poem (eg *Don't Interrupt!* by Demetroulla Vassili or one of the other poems listed above) and either read it aloud or ask a strong reader to do so. Conduct a whole-class discussion on what issue is being raised in the poem. What evidence is there? What is the poet trying to say? How is language used to get the message across?

Homework dealing with the question: 'What is the poet trying to say and how does the poet go about it?'

LINKS WITH CITIZENSHIP

KNOWLEDGE AND UNDERSTANDING ABOUT BECOMING INFORMED CITIZENS

- Pupils learn about the diversity of national, regional, religious and ethnic identities in the United Kingdom and the need for mutual respect and understanding.

- They learn about legal and human rights of citizens.

- They learn the importance of resolving conflict fairly.

- They learn the significance of the media in society.

DEVELOPING SKILLS OF ENQUIRY AND COMMUNICATION

- Pupils learn to think about topical, social and cultural issues, problems and events using and analysing information from different sources.

- They express and justify their personal opinion about such issues, problems and events.

- They contribute to group and exploratory class discussions.

DEVELOPING SKILLS OF PARTICIPATION AND RESPONSIBLE ACTION

- Pupils learn to use their imagination to understand other people's experiences and be able to think about and discuss views that are not their own.

- They take part responsibly in group activities.

English/citizenship, Key Stage 4
TITLE: 'Examination Day' by Henry Slesar

TIME REQUIRED: A double lesson plus preparation

AIMS AND OBJECTIVES

For citizenship:

- To understand that education is a political issue and that there is a need to question what is being taught and why.

For English:

- To read a short story and use it to introduce some of the analytical skills required at Key Stage 4.

- To recognize aspects of the science fiction genre.

- To introduce how Key Stage 4 classes operate on mutual respect and trust and that pupils' ideas/views are valued.

- Allow and encourage pupils to question and analyse texts.

- To use prediction as a skill to question texts and consider how writers surprise their readers and develop suspense.

Background

This section describes a double lesson to introduce English at GCSE and the importance of pupils thinking for themselves.

Examination Day is a science fiction short story (from *NEAB Anthology*, 1996). A young boy's birthday is approaching but this seems to be causing his parents concern. He is asked to sit a government-set examination. We hear the beginning of the test and the questions seem easy. His parents receive a telephone call telling them that he was too clever and asking them where they want him to be buried.

Introduction

Why do children need to be educated? (Reasons might include jobs/personal fulfilment/employment/technology, etc). What should be taught and why? What is it that we have to study? Outline the GCSE requirements asking pupils to question aspects of the course, eg poetry from other cultures. Stress that the coursework element will not just give them marks but skills. Also explain that speaking and listening is worth 30 per cent of their English GCSE; engaging with and sharing ideas and supporting and encouraging each other is therefore important to achieving a good grade.

Development

Ask pupils to listen carefully (perhaps using drafting books to take notes) as they will be asked to predict what happens next. Stop several times for quick brainstorms then take three or four views.

Read to the end of the story. It is a shocking end. What do the pupils find shocking? Is it the deliberate 'dumbing down' of society, or that government is uncaring and all powerful?

As a class, look back at the story to find clues to governmental power and clues to how the story will end (eg the parents' concern).

Explain that for GCSE we should not just be looking for evidence but that we need to have a detailed look at the choice of language and its effect on the reader.

Implications/conclusion

Reinforce the need to question and to keep an open mind. Explain that respect for peers/teachers is the required norm but that a questioning approach is expected. Reflect upon the role and form of government and consider the legal and human rights and responsibilities underpinning society.

LINKS WITH CITIZENSHIP

KNOWLEDGE AND UNDERSTANDING ABOUT BECOMING INFORMED CITIZENS

- Pupils learn about the legal and human rights relating to citizens.

- They learn about the responsibilities of democratic government and of the individual.

- They learn about the role of government in legislation.

DEVELOPING SKILLS OF ENQUIRY AND COMMUNICATION

- Pupils learn to think critically about what they read or are told and to question not assume.

- They learn to express their opinions in the class group.

DEVELOPING SKILLS OF PARTICIPATION AND RESPONSIBLE ACTION

- Pupils learn to use their imagination to consider other people's experiences and to be able to understand and explain those views even if they are not their own.

- They take part responsibly in class discussions.

English/citizenship, Key Stage 4
TITLE: The influence of the media and importance of a free press

TIME REQUIRED: Two or three lessons plus preparation, research time for pupils and homework

AIMS AND OBJECTIVES

For citizenship:

- To consider the legal and human rights and responsibilities underpinning society.

- To consider the work of Parliament, government and courts in making and shaping law.

- To develop speaking and listening skills, contributing to group and class discussions, expressing and justifying personal views.

For English:

- To highlight the difference between the ways tabloid and broadsheet newspapers cover issues.

- To improve pupils' understanding of newspapers considering their task, their audience and purpose and how it affects the language and presentation of newspapers.

- To develop writing skills to argue and persuade in preparation for English paper 1.

- To produce a piece of media coursework for GCSE folders.

- To develop a speaking and listening assessment for GCSE purposes.

Introduction

This group of lessons uses newspaper coverage of topical issues to explore media coverage and to prompt research and debate about the issues. It should culminate in a piece of coursework for their GCSE folder.

Discussion

Circulate copies of broadsheet and tabloid articles about current topics (for example: Stephen Lawrence, euthanasia, Northern Ireland, anarchist riots, civil wars or conflicts or refugee policy in Britain). The Web site www.webwombat.com gives access to recent UK and international newspaper articles and can be searched for specific subjects (see page 34). Hold class discussions about the slants, or newspaper presentation of different issues. This will help to develop close reading skills.

Development

Ask pupils to research a topic, including using the Internet, and be ready to present it to the class. They could present from a particular viewpoint; for example, if they chose to look at the asylum seekers' issue, individuals or groups could put forward the case as seen by refugee families, Amnesty and other pro-human rights organizations, the Home Office, communities where refugees are housed or local councils.

Pupils should then be asked to write a letter expressing their point of view as if for publication in a newspaper of their choice.

Pupils should look at how letters are written and consider whether their letters would appear in one issue or as part of a sequence. They will need to consider task, audience and purpose, their choice of language to persuade and the strength of feeling of the writer.

Implications/conclusion

This class discussion, sharing of research information and written expressions of opinions can be assessed for speaking and listening and could be used as the input for the letters and written part of coursework. For this writing to form part of a GCSE folder, it will be necessary for pupils to demonstrate close reading skills. They should, therefore, have explored the effectiveness of at least two newspaper articles. A commentary explaining their letter would also help assessment.

LINKS WITH CITIZENSHIP

KNOWLEDGE AND UNDERSTANDING ABOUT BECOMING INFORMED CITIZENS

- Pupils learn about the role of the media in shaping and forming public opinion and how they do that.

- They learn about the importance of freedom of the press.

- They learn about the workings of government in the context of the issues in the media at the time.

DEVELOPING SKILLS OF ENQUIRY AND COMMUNICATION

- Pupils learn to examine topical issues from different viewpoints.

- They learn to express their views in class and in writing.

DEVELOPING SKILLS OF PARTICIPATION AND RESPONSIBLE ACTION

- Pupils learn to examine different views of the same news story and evaluate the differences while forming their own opinion.

- They recognize that opposing views may be legitimately held.

- They learn to participate in class discussions.

CHAPTER 6

MATHS

The logical basis of mathematics might lead one to surmise that there is no citizenship learning to be obtained from the study of mathematics. However there is high value in the range of issues dealt with in the study of maths. It can help to develop the skills required to be an active and responsible citizen, even if issues of political democracy, or concepts of community, etc are not directly addressed.

Children and adults are constantly bombarded with all sorts of data in all sorts of forms; sometimes as lists, in tables, in graphs and often within the media as statements of fact. Statistics are part of today's and tomorrow's world and need to be understood – just as there is a need to be literate. Statistics are used in all walks of life whether it is on the latest opinion poll, the differences in house prices throughout the country, the birth rates in various countries, and so on. The list is endless.

The skills required to deal with this mass of statistical information include concepts of analysis, appreciation of number, logic, proof and even the recognition of truth. Without these skills pupils will not be able to differentiate effectively between truth and falsehood or, more prosaically, between statistics and 'damned lies'. In order that we take our part in society we need to have the necessary skills to be able to make informed decisions and choices based on the facts available.

An understanding of number is crucial to daily life, can empower choice and prevent being cheated.

This chapter contains the following activities:

- Key Stage 3

    – *A flexible and extendable series of lessons on the collection and interpretation of data.*

    – *In addition we have described (at the end of the chapter, after Key Stage 4) a weekend of maths activities for Key Stage 3. Although there are advantages to concentrating on the subject over a weekend, many of the activities could be adapted for use in shorter lessons.*

■ Key Stage 4

  – *A series of four or five lessons designed to explore the relationship between variables using scatter diagrams, correlation and prediction.*

  – *Some suggestions on money management for inclusion in key skills work on the application of number. (Also suitable for Key Stage 3.)*

Maths/citizenship, Key Stage 3
TITLE: The use of data

TIME REQUIRED: A series of several lessons that can be expanded according to need

AIMS AND OBJECTIVES

For citizenship:

■ To practise skills of information gathering, analysis and interpretation.

■ To generate logical opinions on the subjects explored and have these expressed and defended.

■ To learn about local government and the public services offered.

For maths:

■ To specify a problem, plan how to approach it and collect data about it.

■ To process the gathered data effectively.

■ To practise ways of representing data, interpreting and discussing results.

Introduction

Pupils need to draw conclusions based on raw numerical data provided by local government departments on a clearly identified topic. Central government figures and statistics could be used and are generally openly available through departmental Web sites, but local government is probably more accessible and may be more relevant to the pupils within the community.

Activity

Pupils/individuals contact the appropriate local government department for figures/statistics. These can be about a wide range of subjects or services but might, for example, be based on what figure is spent on a local public amenity, such as a leisure centre, and how it is funded.

Once the figures/statistics have been received, this is put into a format that is appropriate for analysis. (It is important to bear in mind that the figures will not come in this format, and that teacher input is vital in helping to steer the conclusions drawn in the light of the information available!)

One conclusion might be that 'The local leisure centre is wholly funded by the prices paid by customers'. In order to reach such a conclusion pupils would need to have gathered and analysed data on: running costs (heating/lighting/utilities); staffing costs; repair and maintenance; contingency; entry fee charges; and figures relating to usage.

The data can be used in a number of different mathematical ways, for example:

- simple arithmetical calculations of the relationships between the figures;

- using computers to produce spreadsheets and carry out the calculations;

- using these spreadsheets to produce charts such as pie charts, bar charts, linear graphs and scatter diagrams;

- the calculation of averages (mean, median, mode) and range.

This activity could be expanded to include an environmental slant looking at, for example, how environmentally friendly a local government department is by analysing its spending on issues such as recycling, energy saving, etc. Another possibility would be to look at the funding of local, national or international pressure groups or charities.

Further development

In all of this work there must be some discussion about the use and abuse of statistics. Statistics are about the manipulation of figures and the presentation of them to the public to aid understanding. The question should be asked as to whether some manipulation to provide diagrams, charts, graphs, etc is misleading or acceptable. This theme could be developed to explore whether there might be a deliberate attempt to mislead by the media or by a particular pressure group, for example.

A way to develop this work is to take government statistics about their achievements in areas such as unemployment, average earnings, poverty, or health service waiting lists and examine the way the data is presented, how it would be affected if different measures were taken or classes of data excluded. Perhaps this might be most effectively done at the time of local or national elections to see how different parties interpret the same basic data. Alternatively, detailed research through the media and the Internet could produce different interpretations from the same basic sets of data if the assumptions made about how the information is collated were changed.

LINKS WITH CITIZENSHIP

(Depending upon the actual data and subject used.)

KNOWLEDGE AND UNDERSTANDING ABOUT BECOMING INFORMED CITIZENS

- Pupils learn about the functions of central and local government, the public services they offer and how they are financed, and the opportunities to contribute.

- They learn about the work of community-based, national and international voluntary groups.

- They learn the significance of the media in society.

continued overleaf

continued

DEVELOPING SKILLS OF ENQUIRY AND DEBATE

- Pupils learn to think about topical political, cultural and social issues, problems and events by analysing information from various sources, including ICT-based sources.

- They contribute to group and exploratory class discussions and express their own opinions.

Maths/citizenship, Key Stage 4
TITLE: The relationship between two variables

TIME REQUIRED: A series of three lessons plus preparation

AIMS AND OBJECTIVES

For citizenship:

- To increase pupils' awareness and understanding of statistics.

For maths:

- To introduce pupils to the concept of relationships, link, scatter, correlation/no correlation and line of best fit.

Lesson 1

Introduction

Give each pair of pupils a pair of variables, written on a card. Pupils to discuss whether a relationship exists between the two. If so, what is the link? (It may be necessary to demonstrate with an example using the whole class for ideas.) Pupils then swap once and repeat with another card. Examples of cards:

- numbers of days absent from school and marks in tests;
- amount of light and time taken to fall asleep;
- length and weight of vans;
- length of pregnancy and weight of baby;
- number of years in education and income;
- height of bed from floor and amount of sleep.

Have a brief discussion, as a class, of pupils' findings.

Main activity

Pupils complete their copies of Table 6.1 using data from some of the pupils. At least ten sets of data are required in each table. Pupils are then introduced to the scatter diagram/graph. This is used to show whether there is a link relationship between two sets of data. Pupils enter the data on to scatter graphs with suitable scales.

Examine the graphs and hold a class discussion bringing out such points as:

- What types of relationship exist?
- Did the graphs show what you expected?
- Do you know which cross is for which member of the class?
- What could this type of graph be used for?
- Is the relationship a 'definite' one?

Table 6.1

Name											
Height (cm)											
Hand span (cm)											

Name											
Height (cm)											
Time watching TV last night (hours)											

Name											
Time spent on homework (min)											
Time watching TV last night (hours)											

Table 6.2

Pupil	A	B	C	D	E	F	G	H	I	J	K	L
Maths test mark	42	43	54	58	45	47	52	59	60	53	53	55
Science test mark	36	34	40	48	34	40	38	44	46	38	44	a

a represents absence.

Lesson 2

Introduction

Issue pairs of pupils with a worksheet containing the whole list of pairs of variables from the cards used in Lesson 1. Ask the pupils to sort them into two groups. Bring the class together and discuss the pupils' findings. (Generally they will be sorted into those with a relationship and those without.) Discuss the possibility of subdividing the group with a relationship into smaller groups.

Main activity

Draw appropriate scatter diagrams and introduce pupils to the mathematical terms and concepts of positive and negative correlation and no correlation.

Pupils to give examples of positive, negative and no correlation from the worksheet used during the introduction. They then work on practising these skills using a variety of questions involving scatter graphs.

Recap the main points of correlation, asking pupils to give examples of different types of variables. Ask pupils for any connections that surprised them.

Lesson 3

Introduction

Issue pupils with Table 6.2. Ask the class to draw up a scatter graph of the results. Discuss what to do about pupil L, who was absent for the science test.

Main activity

Introduce pupils to the idea of a 'line of best fit' being a line drawn through the middle of the points on a scatter diagram if there is any correlation. Discuss suitable descriptions for different degrees of scatter around the line of best fit. Issue pupils with examples to practise drawing in lines of best fit.

Discuss methods to show the accuracy of the line. Bring out the importance of the line being as close as possible to the points, of the need for the same number of points above and below the line (suggest pupils use a ruler or piece of thread to help).

Introduce the idea that a line of best fit can be used to estimate one measurement, given the other. Relate this to pupil L in the introduction. Get pupils to draw in the line of best fit for the maths and science test marks. Ask pupils to suggest a science result for pupil L, using their line of best fit and discuss the accuracy of such predictions.

Issue pupils with questions to practise their skills in drawing lines of best fit and estimation from the line.

Recap the main concepts of the lesson and return to the prediction for pupil L. Ask pupils to comment on the advantages and disadvantages of this to predict test results for pupils who are absent for tests. Would they be happy for this method to be used for them?

Lessons 4/5

Introduction

Explain that these two lessons will examine relationships between statistics from government.

Main activity

Pupils are to research statistics from government sources such as the following paired variables:

- base interest rate/inflation rate;

- inflation rate/level of UK unemployment;

- level of UK unemployment/value of imports;

- base interest rate/number of failing firms;

- value of imports/value of exports.

Pupils' research can use several sources including the media and the Internet. Pupils use their skills from the previous lessons to find out whether there is a relationship between the pairs of variables.

Implications

It is important that pupils gain the knowledge to enable them to interpret correctly the true results from graphs showing data analysis. All too often statistics are used in a misleading way with the intention of persuading people to a certain opinion. In order that we take our part in society we need to have the necessary skills to be able to make informed decisions and choices based on the facts available.

LINKS WITH CITIZENSHIP

KNOWLEDGE AND UNDERSTANDING ABOUT BECOMING INFORMED CITIZENS

■ Pupils learn about aspects of the UK economy.

DEVELOPING SKILLS OF ENQUIRY AND COMMUNICATION

■ Pupils learn to research for information from a variety of sources.

■ They learn to interpret statistical information and use statistical techniques for the presentation of information.

■ They learn to interpret statistics using graphs and other data presentation media.

■ They develop numerical and interpretive skills to help make informed decisions and choices.

Maths/citizenship, Key Stage 4
TITLE: Money management

TIME REQUIRED: Parts of key skills lessons on the application of number

AIMS AND OBJECTIVES

For citizenship:

- To learn about aspects of the economy and financial services.

- To experience the media and the Internet as information providers.

For maths:

- To develop mathematical skills of the application of number.

- To gain an understanding of the use of numbers and statistics.

Introduction

A section of work on domestic budgeting could be incorporated into work on key skills and the application of number. There are a variety of short topics using issues of responsible domestic budgeting as the basis for work on number and mathematical skills. A suggested list for use under a general heading of 'Money Management' includes:

■ Credit cards	how they work and a comparison of interest rates on different cards/suppliers
■ Bank accounts	how they work
■ Loans	how the interest rate works
■ Electricity/gas	the difference between fixed charge and/or using tariff

- Mobile phones   what different deals are available?

- Income tax   what is it and why and how is it calculated?

- National insurance   what is it and how is it calculated?

- Mortgages   how do various types work?

- Income and expenditure   basic sums around where the money goes – weekly, monthly and yearly bills – basic cash flow.

Research to get information, including use of the Internet. Compare figures and statistics from different sources. Ensure pupils have gained an understanding of information in different forms and from different sources.

LINKS WITH CITIZENSHIP

KNOWLEDGE AND UNDERSTANDING ABOUT BECOMING INFORMED CITIZENS

- Pupils learn about how public and utility services are financed.

- They learn how the economy functions and the role of business and financial services.

DEVELOPING SKILLS OF ENQUIRY AND COMMUNICATION

- Pupils learn to analyse information, draw conclusions from it and base opinions and actions upon those conclusions.

- They learn to think about topical cultural and social issues and economic problems by analysing information from various sources.

- They contribute to group and exploratory class discussions.

DEVELOPING SKILLS OF PARTICIPATION AND RESPONSIBLE ACTION

- Pupils learn to identify views that are not their own over ways of handling finances and balancing income and expenditure.

Maths/citizenship, Key Stage 3
TITLE: Maths weekend

TIME REQUIRED: A weekend plus considerable preparation. Some of the activities could be adapted for classroom use

Introduction

The idea behind the maths weekend is firmly rooted in the 'maths is fun' idea. It is possible to engage and involve pupils in a way that is not so easily done within the confines of a classroom. Although elements such as group work, presentations, displays and investigative work are possible in the curriculum, the biggest constraint is time. At Key Stage 3, most schools probably deliver maths in single periods. With the weekend available, activities can be extended and perhaps more in-depth investigation can occur. Although most of the activities are essentially mathematical in nature, there are several aspects of the weekend which contribute to citizenship learning.

Involvement

This is an activity firmly directed at Key Stage 3 pupils. It has to be a voluntary activity, not only because it is over a weekend, but also because it is extension work. This does not mean to say that it is targeting more able pupils. In fact, pupils of all abilities are able to take part if they so wish and pupils with special educational needs have benefited from this.

Volunteer helpers, in the form of a small number of older pupils, perhaps those who have shown a particular interest in maths and will probably take A-level maths, are a useful addition to the resources available. They form a good link between younger pupils and staff, and the younger pupils respond to them very well.

There is no reason to confine attendance to maths staff; staff from other disciplines can also take part. This will give an extra interesting perspective to both staff and pupils. Some support from the ICT department, a network co-ordinator or similar is very valuable.

Location

The maths weekend is based outside the school. In our example, the pupils stay in a hotel that we have used for some years and they mingle with the other hotel guests, especially at meal times, although many of the mathematical activities take place in a separate annexe.

What happens in a maths weekend?

This is an opportunity for pupils to develop ideas and to work for longer periods of time on maths in its various guises. It is an opportunity also to learn from the experience of staying away from home and working with others. Perhaps the best way to explain ideas is to look at one or two of the sessions in more detail.

The maths trail

This is a familiarization exercise involving mathematical questions and concepts such as bearings, shapes and numbers and takes place shortly after the arrival of the party at the hotel. As is the case with all activities throughout the course of the weekend, this involves pupils working in pairs or small groups, and so increases their social skills.

The adventure game

The adventure game is introduced through a story involving the fictional Vicar of Little Dean who, many years ago, 'invited six people to a meal in the very room in which you are now sitting'. The story is developed and, at the end, the vicar says goodbye to his guests, shakes hands with each one of them and they then shake hands with each other. How many handshakes are there? This is the first problem of the evening, and the pupils, working in pairs, have to solve it. Once they have done this, they can then move on to the next room. Guarding the next room is a member of staff. Before the pupils can enter this room, they must give that member of staff the correct answer. Failure to do so means they go back to the beginning. The session proceeds like this and, when the last problem has been solved, the winning pair has in their possession a series of numbers. This combination opens the locked chest to reveal the treasure of the Vicar of Little Dean. One of the problems to be solved involves use of computers in a particular room. Just in case there are pairs who seem to be getting through the problems too quickly there are additional roving 'nasty' guards who throw them an extra problem to be solved before they may move on. This game addresses many aspects of citizenship and many key skills including communication, improving pupils' own learning, working with others, problem-solving, application of number and ICT skills.

Candle activity

This is a group activity, focusing on loci, which is held out of doors at night. Figure 6.1 illustrates what happens. Each pupil has a night light in a jar. A square is marked out with string. The pupils are divided into four groups and each group lines up along one of the four sides of the square, holding their candles. The first person in each team stands on one of the corners and looks towards the pupil immediately in front of them in a clockwise (or anticlockwise, as long as all choose the same!) direction. This spot is marked with a candle. This pupil

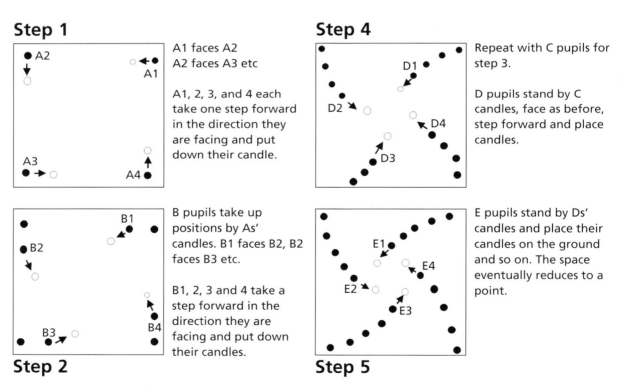

Figure 6.1 The candle game

then takes one step towards the pupil he or she is looking at, marks this spot with a candle and then withdraws. Then the second person in each team goes to this spot, looks towards the appropriate pupil in the right direction, and takes one step toward him or her (this has to be synchronized so that pupils all take the step forward at the same moment). This spot is then marked and the pupil withdraws. By this time the line is beginning to curve and by the time the final pupils have placed their lights they are tightly packed in the middle of the original square and the candles look like a starburst. This provokes much work on loci and on constructions.

The wider picture

As with so many aspects of school life the benefits of the maths weekend are not only in the subject content undertaken. Maths weekends as a whole provide a learning experience for the pupils involved. Another task for pupils to perform during the weekend is the running of the tuck shop.

Tuck shop

A tuck shop is available throughout the weekend. Although the sweets, fruit, drinks, crisps, etc sold here are bought wholesale for the weekend by staff, the rest of the operation is handed over to the pupils. The tuck shop has to be non-profit making and Year 9 pupils use a maths lesson in advance of the weekend to work out the cost of each tuck shop item, using invoices and spreadsheets. Many of the pupils who are involved in this have been on the maths weekend themselves when younger and so identify with the work of producing financial information for the tuck shop. Once the weekend begins teams of pupils, led by the older ones, are responsible for the sale of food at specified times, the financial accounting and liaising with staff to ensure safe custody of the money.

Other benefits

As this is a residential trip there needs to be organization of room-sharing. Pupils are encouraged to sort themselves into single-sex groups who would be happy to share a room; this stage is easy. The next stage, of actually accommodating these groups in appropriately sized rooms, can be more problematic. A group of five 'best friends' may need to split into two groups. This process involves negotiation and some compromise thus helping to develop skills of participation and responsible action.

All the activities of maths weekends involve group work. The pairs/groups involved present the outcomes of their work, perhaps using visual displays. The co-operation needed here, especially over a longer period of time, is a skill that is developed throughout the course of the weekend. This is especially important as many of the groups will involve pupils who do not usually work together.

The weekend is used as an opportunity to identify and reward progress made by pupils. However, care must be taken not to disadvantage those who are unable to attend the weekend. The school's charging policy or the maths department contingency fund will come into play here. Reward can be through the use of certificates to highlight achievement. These fall into a number of categories:

- academic achievement – recognition of noticeable improvement in any particular mathematical area;

- social skills – recognition of achievements in group work, supporting each other, being helpful to school/hotel staff;

- light-hearted awards – these are awarded to the most colourful dresser for example (school uniform is not worn), or the loudest pupil snorer.

Evaluation

Maths weekends are evaluated regularly by both staff and pupils. Staff evaluation has resulted in the extension of the schedule to include activities with a greater range of skills involved. The evaluation by pupils has been carried out by the completion of a diary during the weekend. Another alternative would be to evaluate using a simple questionnaire which should be less time-consuming and which will yield an immediate response at the end of the weekend.

LINKS WITH CITIZENSHIP

KNOWLEDGE AND UNDERSTANDING ABOUT BECOMING INFORMED CITIZENS

- Pupils involved in the tuck shop learn something of how non-profit making concerns operate and the rights of consumers.

DEVELOPING SKILLS OF ENQUIRY AND COMMUNICATION

- Pupils learn how to think about problems, analyse information and its sources, including ICT-based sources.

- They contribute to group and exploratory discussions and take part in debates.

DEVELOPING SKILLS OF PARTICIPATION AND RESPONSIBLE ACTION

- Pupils learn how to negotiate, decide and take part responsibly in school activities (one of the main themes of the whole weekend).

- They learn to reflect on the process of participating (through the evaluation).

CHAPTER 7

SCIENCE

The ever growing importance of scientific issues in our daily lives demands a populace which has sufficient knowledge and understanding to follow science and scientific debates.

Nuffield Foundation (1998, p1)

This quotation sums up the value that science teaching has to add to the understanding of citizenship. How can pupils reasonably debate or hold an opinion on such topical issues as genetic modification, pollution or cloning, to name but a few, without some understanding of what they might mean? Without that understanding, how can the pupil, soon to be an adult citizen, participate responsibly or contribute to the debate about such issues?

The rate at which science is moving on so many fronts will continue to accelerate and the moral dilemmas raised will continue to increase in number. An understanding of basic scientific principles is essential.

Science is moving too fast for there to be any hope of maintaining currency with all that is developing. However, it is vital for science teaching in schools to raise interest in the subject and to offer some basic principles. An additional role for the science teacher to contribute to citizenship learning is to ensure that pupils begin to understand the moral issues that inevitably arise from scientific progress.

In this chapter we include the following activities:

- Key Stage 3

    - *A series of three or four lessons on endangered species and their habitats.*

    - *A group of three lessons on renewable energy sources.*

> – *A group of possible lessons to discuss the ethics of scientific developments.*

■ Key Stage 4

> – *A double lesson (with earlier introduction to get pupils to research the topic) to debate the costs and relative benefits of space exploration.*

> – *Some of the lessons about the ethics of scientific developments (above) are suitable for Key Stage 4.*

Science/citizenship, Key Stage 3
TITLE: Endangered species and their habitats

TIME REQUIRED: A series of three or four lessons, plus research and preparation

AIMS AND OBJECTIVES

For citizenship:

■ To research a global moral issue using a variety of methods.

■ To develop opinions and express them orally and in writing.

For science:

■ To consider the problems of destruction of habitats and the subsequent decline in the numbers of some animals and plants which have become endangered.

Introduction

Hold a class discussion/brainstorm about habitat loss and the reasons for it. Draw out as many as possible of the major reasons, for example more people, more food, more homes, more factories and roads and demand for more raw materials – wood, metal, oil, etc.

Discuss and explain the effects of destroying habitats on the balance of ecosystems. There is an opportunity to explore this concept if it has not already been addressed elsewhere.

Introduce and discuss food chains and predation. Organisms become endangered as numbers fall and they become in danger of extinction.

Development

Brief pupils to undertake a project, either individually or in small groups depending upon the make-up of the class, on an endangered animal or plant. An example is the habitat project below.

HABITAT PROJECT

Many species of animal are being threatened by our use of the planet. Some examples of animals that need our help if they are to survive are giant pandas, elephants and whales.

Find out about one animal and write about it. Your project should include information about where on the Earth the animal lives, what habitat it prefers, what it eats and how it is threatened by our activities. Try to find out about efforts to conserve the animal. Your project will be improved if you add pictures or newspaper cuttings about the animal and take care to present your work well.

Encourage and assist pupils to use some or all of the following for research:

- computers, the Internet and CD ROM;

- libraries for books and newspapers;

- personal contacts; who do they know who has a specific interest – for example, pupils may be members of WWF or subscribe to appropriate magazines; parents or friends may subscribe to wildlife charities.

Encourage pupils/groups to concentrate on the following points:

- Where does it live (countries and particular habitat)?
- Feeding habits – what does it eat?
- Why is it becoming endangered?
- How is it being protected/helped?
- Pictures/newspaper cuttings, etc to reinforce messages.

You may wish to give pupils choices about the way in which their projects are presented. This can be done in a variety of ways, for example: posters; booklets; newspaper articles; speeches in a debate; or simply as an illustrated essay.

Conclusion

In the final lesson of the series, ensure that pupils share their information with the rest of the class. This could be through presentation (verbally or on posters), through reading others' work and discussing the conclusions or in the form of a structured debate.

LINKS WITH CITIZENSHIP

KNOWLEDGE AND UNDERSTANDING ABOUT BECOMING INFORMED CITIZENS

- Pupils learn about the way the world is a global and ecological community, and the political, economic, environmental and social implications of this for our life on the planet.
- They learn about the work of voluntary groups working in conservation.

DEVELOPING SKILLS OF ENQUIRY AND DEBATE

- Pupils learn to think about topical political and social

continued overleaf

continued

issues, problems and events by analysing information from different sources, including ICT and the Internet.

- They learn to express and justify orally and in writing their opinions about such issues and problems.

- They contribute to group and exploratory class discussions.

DEVELOPING SKILLS OF PARTICIPATION AND RESPONSIBLE ACTION

- Pupils learn to take part responsibly in activities, communicating with others both within and outside the school.

- They reflect on the process of participating.

Science/citizenship, Key Stage 3
TITLE: Renewable energy sources

TIME REQUIRED: Three lessons plus preparation

AIMS AND OBJECTIVES

For science and citizenship:

- To research information on renewable energy sources, why we need them and practical ways to use energy more efficiently in daily life.

- To present information to the class using any appropriate medium.

- To consider the benefits and drawbacks of scientific and technological developments, including those related to the environment, health and quality of life.

Introduction

Work that needs to be covered before this lesson includes current world energy sources, the extent to which we rely on these sources and the importance of energy in supporting our current way of life.

Energy is an integral part of the modern Western idea of civilization. Whether it is in terms of heating and cooking, of transport or of manufacturing, we rely heavily on a supply of energy. However, we would be naïve to think that this situation will last forever. There are a number of very pressing reasons why we should review the sources of energy that we use. We should perhaps also review the way that we live our lives to see whether we could be more energy efficient.

Note: All GCSE pupils need to have some understanding of a number of renewable energy sources and their advantages and disadvantages. It would be helpful if the information gathered by individuals and groups during this activity is shared among the class as a whole.

Discussion/activity

Groups of pupils are asked to prepare information packs, covering all the relevant information on one renewable energy source, which is then copied for the rest of the class as their notes for this topic. The groups should explore possible areas to investigate and present, and decide which they wish to tackle.

Discuss possible sources of information. After some preliminary research to establish the exact areas to be covered, groups need to organize themselves to work efficiently; an outline plan of the proposed presentation is an aid to task allocation within the group. Each pupil must contribute (according to his or her strengths) to all parts of the work.

Pupils need to discuss and agree possible ways of presenting the material (information may be presented to the class as posters, verbal presentations, information booklets, video presentations, etc) and the advantages and disadvantages of each. It may be useful to refer to examples of good practice and set levels of expectation at this stage.

Final presentation to the whole group can be assessed for quality and detail of presentation as well as content.

Development

It is important for most syllabuses that pupils have information on a number of renewable sources of energy. Therefore it is important that, although they may have focussed on one, they need to make notes on the others. If other groups covered these alternatives, homework/follow-up activities can be to make notes on the information presented by the other students.

A display of the work produced could be put up for other pupils to see in the form of poster presentations or booklets set out for all to read. Verbal presentations could be made to other groups.

LINKS WITH CITIZENSHIP

KNOWLEDGE AND UNDERSTANDING ABOUT BECOMING INFORMED CITIZENS

- Pupils learn about how the economy functions, including the role of business and financial services.

- They learn about the opportunities for individuals and voluntary groups to bring about social and environmental change locally, nationally, in Europe and internationally.

- They learn about the rights and responsibilities of consumers, employers and employees.

- They learn about the wider issues and challenges of global interdependence and responsibility, including sustainable development.

DEVELOPING SKILLS OF ENQUIRY AND COMMUNICATION

- Pupils learn how to research a topical issue by acquiring and analysing information from different sources, including the Internet, in order to form opinions.

- They learn to express, justify and defend orally and in writing their personal opinion about these issues.

continued

continued

- They learn to contribute to group and exploratory class discussions.

DEVELOPING SKILLS OF PARTICIPATION AND RESPONSIBLE ACTION

- Pupils learn to negotiate, decide and take part responsibly in school activities.

Science/citizenship, Key Stage 3 (with variations suitable for Key Stage 4)

TITLE: Examination of the ethical questions raised by modern scientific developments

---

TIME REQUIRED: One or several lessons plus preparation

These ethical questions are, by their nature, scientific but they have implications far beyond the laboratory and should be discussed by both scientists and the wider public. Therefore these subjects could also be covered by general debates or in PSHE lessons if time is limited in science lessons.

AIMS AND OBJECTIVES

For citizenship:

- To raise awareness of responsibilities which scientists have towards the rest of society.

- To research and discuss topical scientific issues which affect society and come to informed judgements about such issues.

For science:

- To learn how to research information about a scientific subject using the Internet.

■ To gain awareness that the application of science can have far reaching consequences.

Introduction

In advance of the discussion session research must be carried out and resources produced which will stimulate debate. This can be done by the teacher or, preferably, by pupils perhaps as preparatory homework. The Internet is a useful source of up-to-date information and free resources for class discussion (see Chapter 3, page 34 onwards).

Discussion

Pupils study information about a scientific development of topical interest and discuss the wider implications. Often the teacher may play 'devil's advocate' in order to bring about discussion of all aspects of the subject and both sides of the argument.

EXAMPLE: POLLUTION

Do we have the right to pollute our planet or a responsibility to keep it healthy for the sake of all other species? The pollution Web site www.pollution.com is a good starting point to research a huge variety of information about all aspects of the pollution debate.

At the end of the discussion a vote could be taken to establish the opinions of the class.

Development for Key Stage 4

The format used above could also be used for Key Stage 4 lessons. Some examples of possible topics include:

■ 'Dolly' the sheep and the cloning debate. The online newspaper search engine www.webwombat.com (search for cloning), www.humancloning.org and http://physics.syr.edu/courses/modules/BIOLOGY HEALTH provide masses of information about cloning including review articles for scientific publications like *Nature*, *New Scientist* and *Scientific American* which can be used to inform debate.

■ GM foods: benefit or hazard? The Web site www.millennium-debate.org/gmfoods.htm has recent articles from leading British newspapers which can be read on screen or printed for use by the class.

LINKS WITH CITIZENSHIP

KNOWLEDGE AND UNDERSTANDING ABOUT BECOMING INFORMED CITIZENS

■ Pupils learn about the rights and obligations of responsible behaviour in science as elsewhere.

■ They learn about issues of interdependence and global responsibility

■ They learn about the opportunities that individuals and groups have to try to bring about change.

DEVELOPING SKILLS OF ENQUIRY AND COMMUNICATION

■ Pupils learn to research current topics using the Internet and other resources.

■ They develop reasoned opinions based on their research and express those opinions in discussion.

DEVELOPING SKILLS OF PARTICIPATION AND RESPONSIBLE ACTION

■ Pupils learn to see the world from different perspectives and standpoints to be able to justify their own position in the light of opposing views.

■ They take part responsibly in group discussions.

Science/citizenship, Key Stage 4
TITLE: The benefits versus the cost of space exploration, compared with alternative activities such as aid programmes

TIME REQUIRED: A double lesson for the debate plus preparation, beginning several weeks before lessons begin, to marshal information and the cases for debate

AIMS AND OBJECTIVES

For science and citizenship:

- To provide pupils with an opportunity to research the issues surrounding the cost of space exploration, using the Internet.

- To use the research material to consider, debate and arrive at a democratic decision about these issues.

Introduction

Hold a short discussion around the fact that people are starving on our planet yet we spend billions of pounds/dollars on space research. Should we try to improve the lives of people on Earth first? Why do governments spend so much on space projects? Wouldn't it be in their interests to divert money to more immediate/relevant needs? What exactly is space research about? Do we benefit or is it all about satellite TV?

Preparatory work

Pupils in pairs or small groups are briefed to research the cost and benefits of space exploration and the cost and benefits of possible alternative activities, eg aid programmes, with the intention of putting forward an argument for or against the case for space exploration.

Before the day on which the cases are to be put ensure that there are teams with different views and allocate roles for the double lesson debate.

Useful resources

- www.nasa/gov contains plenty of information about what we gain from space exploration.

- www.hq.nasa.gov/office/nsp/appendix/htm details the funding NASA receives from the US government and what their long-term goals are.

- www.oxfam.org.uk allows pupils to find Oxfam's annual review detailing how much money they have to spend in one year and how they spend it.

- www.esrin.esa.it is the Web site of the European Space Agency. Pupils can find out how much Europe and the UK spend on space projects.

- www.star.le.ac.uk is the Space School at Leicester University.

A lot of information can be obtained by telephoning the Space Research Centre on 0116 252 2675 and information packs are available from Oxfam's Education Unit, 4th floor, 4 Bridge Place, London, SW1V 1XY.

Discussion

Either hold a debate or role play a debate.

Debate

Hold a secret ballot of opinion before the debate begins. Ask for speakers to propose and second motions for and against a suitable motion. Allow discussion and debate. Hear the closing speeches and take a closing vote. (See *Developing Citizenship in Secondary Schools*, Chapter 7, by the same authors, for the practicalities of debating.)

Role-playing a debate

Either pupils or the teacher prepare information cards as a result of the research. Ask for pupil volunteers to represent certain interested parties and provide them with relevant information cards.

Structure the debate so that the arguments appear in some logical order. For example:

1. spokesperson on behalf of government, justifying the expenditure;

2. spokesperson on behalf of an aid organization (or government aid programme);

3. spokesperson on behalf of the scientific community;

4. spokesperson on behalf of a developing country in need of aid;

5. spokesperson on behalf of business or the communications industry.

It should be possible to allow members of the audience to participate between speakers. Once again, a vote before and after the debate might be interesting.

Development

■ Pupils write an essay/notes summarizing the points for and against space expenditure and form an opinion; are they for or against the idea of spending money on space exploration?

■ Class writes to the local MP summarizing the points and asking for his or her party's views on the subject.

■ Pupils write an essay/notes discussing the importance of knowing what government is spending our money on, whether it is space exploration or charity work. How can individuals influence governmental thinking on these issues?

LINKS WITH CITIZENSHIP

KNOWLEDGE AND UNDERSTANDING ABOUT BECOMING INFORMED CITIZENS

- Pupils learn about the opportunities for individuals and voluntary groups to bring about social change in different ways in different parts of the world.

- They learn about the importance of a free press and the media's role in society, including the Internet, in providing information and affecting opinion.

- They learn about the wider issues and challenges of global interdependence and responsibility.

DEVELOPING SKILLS OF ENQUIRY AND COMMUNICATION

- Pupils learn to research a topical issue and analyse information from different sources, including the Internet, in order to form an opinion.

- They learn to express, justify and defend orally and in writing their personal opinion about such an issue.

- They learn to contribute to group and exploratory class discussions and take part in formal debates.

DEVELOPING SKILLS OF PARTICIPATION AND RESPONSIBLE ACTION

- Pupils learn to negotiate, decide and take part responsibly in class and school activities.

CHAPTER 8

GEOGRAPHY

Geography can, of course, provide a much wider education than the ability to read maps and recite the capitals of the countries of the world. As with every subject, it should be taught in the wider social context. Care must be taken to remain impartial and put all sides of a case.

Clearly, the study of social geography should include discussion of subjects such as poverty, equality, famine, human rights and similar issues. These discussions will lead to greater understanding of the individual's role and responsibility in being a citizen of the world. This is achieved through respect for diversity and acting in a way that helps to make the world a more equitable place in which to live and one in which life and prosperity can be more readily sustained. Mankind's relationship with his environment must become a serious element in understanding what it is to be a citizen.

The issues described by Walkington (1999) as being central to the teaching of citizenship through geography are shown in Table 8.1.

Table 8.1 Teaching citizenship through geography

Values	Concepts	Skills
A sense of place	Sustainability	Comparison
A sense of community	Interdependence	Critical thinking
Empathy	Change	Decision making
	Place	
	Cultural diversity	

In this chapter we include the following activities:

- Key Stage 3

  - *A two-lesson exercise in local democracy situated around a national park.*

  - *A single lesson to explore the working of the EU.*

- Key Stage 4

  - *Two lessons to look at the Common Agricultural Policy and its impact.*

  - *Two lessons to study deprivation in inner cities.*

Geography/citizenship, Key Stage 3
TITLE: Conflict in national parks

TIME REQUIRED: Two lessons plus preparation

AIMS AND OBJECTIVES

For citizenship and geography:

- To understand how major conflicts or issues are settled by presentation of ideas through a public enquiry.

- To present a detailed argument outlining a specific point of view.

- To listen to other points of view.

- To make an informed decision based on the evidence.

Introduction

Outline the proposal: A theme park is to be built in an old china clay quarry on Dartmoor, an Area of Outstanding Natural Beauty and a national park. A public enquiry is to be held.

Discussion

Ask pupils to brainstorm a list of the various people likely to be involved in or affected by this venture. They should try to identify who are likely to be supporters and who opponents of the proposal. Then divide the class into small groups.

Development

- Each group should choose a different character/role and discuss the arguments he or she would put forward.

- Each group should write a speech that one person from the group will deliver on the day of the enquiry.

- Before the 'enquiry' gets underway, choose a chairperson who will run the public enquiry.

- Run the public enquiry on formal lines using the usual rules of debate, eg speaking and listening. (See *Developing Citizenship in Secondary Schools* by the same authors, Chapter 7 for rules of debate.)

- Obtain the judgement of the enquiry.

- Take a vote to find out if the class agrees with the decision of the enquiry.

Extension work

Examine the process of a public enquiry and see if it is a fair and just way of deciding sensitive issues. Consider other ways of collective decision-making eg referenda. Pupils may need to research these topics before a well-informed discussion could be held.

LINKS WITH CITIZENSHIP

KNOWLEDGE AND UNDERSTANDING ABOUT BECOMING INFORMED CITIZENS

- Pupils learn about legal and human rights and responsibilities underpinning society.

- They learn about central and local government functions and the public services they offer.

- They learn about the political, economic, environmental and social implications of decision-making in the national and local community.

DEVELOPING SKILLS OF ENQUIRY AND COMMUNICATION

- Pupils learn to think about political and social issues, problems and events by analysing information from a variety of sources.

- They learn to express and justify a personal opinion orally and in writing.

- They learn to contribute to group and exploratory class discussions and take part in debates.

DEVELOPING SKILLS OF PARTICIPATION AND RESPONSIBLE ACTION

- Pupils learn to use their imagination to consider other people's experiences and be able to think about, express and explain views that are not their own.

- They learn to negotiate, decide and take part responsibly in school-based activities.

Geography/citizenship, Key Stage 3
TITLE: Understanding the working of the European Union

TIME REQUIRED: One lesson plus preparation

AIMS AND OBJECTIVES

For citizenship and geography:

- To know who initiated the European Union (EU).

- To know which European countries are member states.

- To understand the reasons for working together.

- To understand the various functions performed by the European Union.

Introduction

Discuss the term 'EU ' and what it means. Introduce key words or terms, eg 'federation of states', 'Common Market', the 'Euro', 'single currency', 'MEP'.

Tasks

- Construct a map to show original and newer members of the European Union.

- Locate on the map Brussels, Strasbourg, The Hague and other capital cities.

- Discuss why Brussels, Strasbourg and The Hague are locations for important EU functions. Develop this with a description of the major EU institutions, their purpose and location.

Development

Encourage pupils to bring in newspaper articles or news reports on various aspects of the work of the EU, focussing on its successes and failures. Discuss these in class before setting out the research element of the lessons.

Ask pupils to use suitable resources to find out which functions the EU performs. (Some EU Web sites are described at the end of this book. The main Web site can be found at http://europa.eu.int.) Get them to look in more detail at the Common Agricultural Policy (CAP) or the Court of Human Rights or the European Parliament. Individual elements should be addressed by different groups of pupils. This would provide a research element and could be either a class-time activity or homework based. An oral presentation could be given to the class by the different groups to ensure all the class have some understanding of all the issues researched.

LINKS WITH CITIZENSHIP

KNOWLEDGE AND UNDERSTANDING ABOUT BECOMING INFORMED CITIZENS

Depending on specific topics researched pupils learn about:

■ the key characteristics of parliamentary and other forms of government;

■ the electoral system and the importance of voting;

■ the world as a global community and the political, economic, environmental and social implications of this, and the role of the EU within that.

DEVELOPING SKILLS OF ENQUIRY AND COMMUNICATION

■ Pupils learn to think about topical political, cultural and social issues, problems and events by analysing information and its sources.

■ They learn to contribute to group and exploratory class discussion.

■ They learn to contribute to a presentation of information researched.

Geography/citizenship, Key Stage 4
TITLE: The Common Agricultural Policy and its consequences

TIME REQUIRED: Two lessons plus preparation

RESOURCES REQUIRED: *Understanding GCSE Geography* by Ann Bowen and John Pallister (1999)

AIMS AND OBJECTIVES

For citizenship and geography:

- To understand the role of the EU in British farming, ie the aims of the Common Agricultural Policy (CAP).

- To understand the language of the CAP, eg quotas, subsidies and price support, and how they affect farming.

- To understand the concept of overproduction and the appearance of 'grain mountains' and 'liquid lakes'.

- To understand the environmental impact of such policies.

- To understand how these policies have changed the farming landscape in Britain.

Introduction

Briefly set the scene by describing the main provisions of the CAP and set it against the background of arable farming in the UK and changes that have taken place within the arable farm.

Discussion

Either as a class or in small groups, who later share information in the whole class, discuss whether or not the aims of the CAP are fair? What are the effects of the CAP on farmers and on the environment?

Development

- Describe the aims of the CAP and whom they most benefit.

- Explain the pricing policies and subsidies.

- Describe the effects of CAP under the following subheadings:

    - *environmental effects;*

    - *overproduction;*

    - *the changes on farms.*

Extension work

Ask pupils to discuss or research whether or not the CAP has been beneficial to British farming. This work could be approached from the viewpoint of the costs and benefits of the CAP.

LINKS WITH CITIZENSHIP

KNOWLEDGE AND UNDERSTANDING ABOUT BECOMING INFORMED CITIZENS

- Pupils learn about the functions of government and the EU and the United Kingdom's relations with the EU.

DEVELOPING SKILLS OF ENQUIRY AND COMMUNICATION

- Pupils learn to research topical issues using different sources and methods.

- They learn to express and justify opinions formed on the basis of their enquiries.

Geography/citizenship, Key Stage 4
TITLE: Inner city investigation. Testing the hypothesis that the inner city is disadvantaged compared with other areas of the city

TIME REQUIRED: Two lessons plus preparation, and homework

RESOURCES REQUIRED

- *Key Geography Connections* by David Waugh (1991).

- *Understanding GCSE Geography* by Ann Bowen and John Pallister (1999).

- Census data. Obviously, pupils will find local examples from cities close to their location most relevant. Any appropriate inner-city census figures can be used.

AIMS AND OBJECTIVES

For citizenship:

- To extrapolate from census data information to support the concept of deprivation.

- To understand the use of social and economic indicators of wealth and deprivation.

- To gather information to support or reject the hypothesis.

- To use graphical techniques to show results.

For geography:

- To understand the deprivation that exists within an inner-city area.

- To understand the reasons for this deprivation.

Introduction

Explain the historical background around the concept of an inner city and its characteristics.

Development

Differentiated work is appropriate here. More able pupils could use the census data and text books to compile a report, using a variety of graphical techniques, to accept or reject the hypothesis. The less able pupils could work through a carefully structured worksheet.

Encourage pupils to look at pictures of the inner-city areas in the nineteenth century, and then maps and statistics of land use and environmental quality in the inner city by the early 1980s or later if available. Differences are easily identified. Pupils should then be able to write a brief summary of their findings and argue whether the hypothesis should be rejected or accepted.

LINKS WITH CITIZENSHIP

KNOWLEDGE AND UNDERSTANDING ABOUT BECOMING INFORMED CITIZENS

- Pupils learn about the social effects of economics and business in action.

DEVELOPING SKILLS OF ENQUIRY AND COMMUNICATION

- Pupils learn to research topical issues using statistics to generate opinions.
- They learn to present statistics effectively to support a case.
- They learn to express and justify an opinion.

DEVELOPING SKILLS OF PARTICIPATION AND RESPONSIBLE ACTION

- Pupils learn to understand and empathize with the experiences of others.

CHAPTER 9

HISTORY

History provides an excellent opportunity to teach citizenship. Whatever the period being studied there will be rich ground for the exploration of the development of democracy, of the pursuit of liberty and freedom of speech, individual human rights and the rights and duties of a citizen. The development of these can be tracked through history and used to draw comparisons with those of today and to stimulate debate about what life would be like under different regimes and different governmental systems. Political literacy is a key outcome from the study of history.

History also provides opportunities for research, for enquiry into the past using original materials from the time. This allows interpretation, the consideration of different possible explanations and the development of the critical appraisal of 'fact' in the examination of different versions of history. All these are key enabling skills for citizenship.

A useful resource might be The Public Record Office www.pro.gov.uk/education who provide a number of resources for lessons, particularly in history, for Key Stages 3 and 4, some of which will be relevant for citizenship.

In this chapter we provide the following activities:

- Key Stage 3

  - *A single lesson to examine the evolution of wider voting rights using the Chartists' six points.*

  - *A series of four lessons to explore the roles and duties of citizenship in Ancient Rome and draw comparisons with citizens today in Britain.*

- Key Stage 4

  A series of five lessons and course work around a visit to a historical site.

History/citizenship, Key Stage 3
TITLE: The Chartists' six points

TIME REQUIRED: Single lesson plus preparation

AIMS AND OBJECTIVES

For citizenship:

■ To understand the issues of emancipation in the Chartist demands in the nineteenth century and to see these in a modern context.

For history:

■ To appreciate the reasons behind the Chartists' demands.

■ To understand what these demands entailed.

■ To compare with conditions in the twentieth and twenty-first centuries.

Introduction

This is teacher led with appropriate texts/visual aids.

■ Put the Chartists in the context of the 1832 Reform Act, ie it enfranchized the middle class (not artisan or working class) and so disappointed many.

■ Put the Act in the context of the political system of the time:

   – *an open ballot and bullying/corruption at elections;*

   – *no payment for MPs;*

   – *inequality of size and representation in electoral areas;*

> – *inequality in those entitled to vote (based on money);*
>
> – *MPs needing property in order to stand.*

Discussion

In groups/pairs set up a discussion about what implications these issues have for representation of the ordinary people.

Groups report back on what additional reforms they would like to see. This will result in either the Chartist demands being identified or provide a useful base to bring out the Chartist demands.

Note: The most likely demand to be missed will be that for annual parliaments and this will provoke its own discussion.

Development

This to be teacher led and aimed towards the creation of a timeline of events by pupils.

- Look at the achievement of five out of six demands, ie 1867 Reform Act, 1872 Secret Ballot Act and the 1884 Reform Act.

- Look at significant omissions, eg votes for women and for those who did not own property.

Implications for today

- Class to compile reasons why the success of the Chartist demands is still significant today. This can be through a class brainstorm or small groups producing lists to share.

- Discussion of twentieth/twenty-first century factors, ie votes for women, lowering of the age of voting.

Conclusion

- What have we learned?

- Is this important in today's world?

LINKS WITH CITIZENSHIP

KNOWLEDGE AND UNDERSTANDING ABOUT BECOMING INFORMED CITIZENS

- Pupils learn about the legal and human rights underpinning society.

- They learn about the key characteristics of parliamentary and other forms of government.

- They learn about the electoral process and the significance of voting.

- They learn about the importance of resolving conflict fairly.

DEVELOPING SKILLS OF ENQUIRY AND COMMUNICATION

- Pupils learn to think about topical political issues and the development of democracy and universal franchise.

- They justify their personal opinion about these issues.

- They contribute to group and exploratory class discussions.

DEVELOPING SKILLS OF PARTICIPATION AND RESPONSIBLE ACTION

- Pupils learn to use their imagination to consider other people's experiences through an attempt to see what it might mean not to have a vote even after electoral reform.

- They learn to take part responsibly in group activities and discussions.

History/citizenship, Key Stage 3
TITLE: The Roman Republic

TIME REQUIRED: Four lessons plus preparation

AIMS AND OBJECTIVES

For citizenship:

- To explore the development of democracy and how it is practised.

For history:

- To introduce the idea of the government of Rome and the role of the citizen.

Lesson 1

- Ask pupils to brainstorm on the subject 'What different jobs are there within the school community?'

- Pupils to construct an organization chart indicating the variety of roles within a school, ie pupils, governors, teachers, parents, year councils, etc.

- Discuss the responsibilities of the groups/individuals in the chart.

- Outline the development of Rome from a kingdom to a republic. Refer to the reign of Tarquin the Proud and introduce the concept of the Roman citizen.

- Explain the importance of the responsibilities and rights of Roman citizens and how the political system was organized and the roles and ranks of different groups of people. Ask pupils to draw up a chart describing this; this will be used in the next lesson.

Lesson 2

This is a role play in which the classroom becomes the Roman assembly. The role-played discussions will form the basis for a debate in the next lesson.

- Pupils become citizens, ie patricians, consuls, magistrates, plebeians, tribunes, members of the Senate. For this activity the chart describing the responsibilities and rights of Roman citizens, compiled in the previous lesson, will be needed in order that pupils can get into role.

- Pupils need to:

    - *identify their roles;*

    - *gather together in groups of pupils with the same role;*

    - *in their groups, and in the role of their chosen citizen type, discuss the same significant issue within each group (this could be corruption during the elections, giving more land to the poor or raising taxation to fund military activities for instance);*

    - *make notes on the discussion.*

Lesson 3

Hold a formal class debate in the assembly based upon the previous lesson's issue.

After the debate pupils should be asked to write/wordprocess a newspaper account of the proceedings. At this point make reference to who was excluded from citizenship in Rome.

Lesson 4

Citizens in Britain today: a comparison with the rights and duties of citizens in Rome. Look at democracy, election, representation and citizenship.

LINKS WITH CITIZENSHIP

KNOWLEDGE AND UNDERSTANDING ABOUT BECOMING INFORMED CITIZENS

- Pupils learn about legal and human rights and responsibilities underpinning society.

- They learn about the role of government and how democratic forums affect the actions of government.

- They learn about the key characteristics of parliamentary and other forms of representative government.

- They learn about the electoral system and the significance of voting.

DEVELOPING SKILLS OF ENQUIRY AND COMMUNICATION

- Pupils learn to think about political, social and cultural issues.

- They learn to express and justify their personal opinion orally and in writing .

- They contribute to group and exploratory class discussions and take part in debates.

DEVELOPING SKILLS OF PARTICIPATION AND RESPONSIBLE ACTION

- Pupils use their imagination to consider other people's experiences as they try to identify with the roles of various Roman citizens with their rights and responsibilities.

- They reflect on the process of participating and its similarities to representative debate in parliament or the Roman Forum.

History/citizenship, Key Stage 4
TITLE: A local study: Aquae Sulis

TIME REQUIRED: A series of five lessons, plus preparation, and a day visit to a local historical site. The example given is that of the Roman baths at Aquae Sulis (Bath) but the principle could be adapted to historical sites local to individual schools

RESOURCES: Local Tourist Board material should be available for most major sites. In this example we used *The Roman Baths, A View over 2000 Years* by Barry Cunliffe

AIMS AND OBJECTIVES

For citizenship:

■ To practise skills of enquiry, research and participation.

For history:

■ To understand the importance of Aquae Sulis in Roman times.

■ To appreciate how Aquae Sulis changed during the Roman occupation.

Introduction

The lessons aim to address the history of Aquae Sulis in the period under discussion and to prepare pupils for the production of two coursework essays.

Lesson 1

Aim: To remind pupils of the context within which Aquae Sulis was built, ie Roman Britain.

Introduction

- Ask pupils to brainstorm what they can remember of Roman Britain from Key Stage 3. Experience has shown that pupils' memories are likely to centre around the key words 'army', 'Roman roads',' villas', 'hypocausts' and 'gods/goddesses'.

- Use these as a starting point to build up a picture. If the army has cropped up it is easy then to begin with the invasion of Britain in AD 43. If it has not the teacher will need to prompt.

- Once the Roman invasion has been introduced, look at the desire of those who had arrived and were now in control to recreate certain aspects of Roman lifestyle in Britain.

- Mention of climatic differences between Britain and Italy and the Romans' desire for cleanliness should lead to discussion of hypocausts, villas and public baths.

Development

- Using appropriate maps, look at the geographical location of the site that was to become Aquae Sulis and discuss the value of its natural feature, the continuous spring of hot mineral water in the centre of Bath.

- In small groups or pairs, the pupils discuss the reasons for building the baths at Aquae Sulis.

Lessons 2 and 3

Aim: To ensure pupils have an understanding of the purposes and mechanics of the public baths.

Introduction

- Compare the Roman baths with perhaps its nearest modern equivalent, a leisure centre.

- In pairs or small groups pupils identify the various reasons for going to a leisure centre. Usually the reasons suggested are fitness, to take part in activities for pleasure, to socialize, as a status symbol (if it is a high-profile gym).

- Compare these reasons with reasons for going to the public baths in the Roman Empire.

- Then draw out the major differences, ie that Romans used the baths primarily to keep clean. The baths were an aid to public health accessible to all citizens. In addition there were temples within the complex, so a visit to the baths also had a religious element.

Development

- Look in detail at the layout of the rooms in a typical public baths and their specific functions. This brings in the use of key terms which need to be explained in context, such as 'frigidarium', 'tepidarium' and 'caldarium'.

- Look at plans for the public baths complex in Aquae Sulis to familiarize pupils with the layout.

- Take a detailed look at the religious buildings and discuss their purposes. Introduce the concept of a polytheistic society and the importance, to the Romans, of worshipping gods who had specific responsibilities. Look at the Romans' tolerance of other societies and their gods and their willingness to adopt/ amalgamate local gods with their own, eg Sulis Minerva.

- Look at the other reasons why Aquae Sulis was an important site, ie defence, a possible civitas, economic and transport/communications importance.

Lesson 4

Aim: To prepare pupils for a site visit and ensure they make the best use of this invaluable opportunity to learn about Aquae Sulis and collect information which will help them write their coursework essays.

Introduction

Stress that pupils need to use all opportunities on their day site visit to find out as much information as possible relating to the essay questions. This will mean:

- Completing worksheets given out prior to the visit. These direct pupils towards important buildings, artefacts and remains and ask key questions which the pupils need to answer.

- Going round the site using the audio guide.

- Taking notes at the taught sessions given by the guides, who are experts in their fields, and asking pertinent questions of the guide during the guided tour.

- Making careful observations of the site and preserving a record for later use by taking photographs, making sketches, buying postcards, guidebooks, etc.

- Reading the inscriptions on military tombstones, altars, curses, signs, etc and using these in appropriate places in their essays.

- Looking at religious imagery, statues, gifts to the gods , etc and using these for their essays.

- Discussing what they find or think with teachers accompanying the visit and with peers.

Lesson 5

This takes place after the visit to the baths and pupils use this lesson to evaluate their findings and identify which pieces of information will be appropriate for each essay. There should be discussion of the problems of collecting and evaluating evidence. Many of these will have become apparent from the visit and include:

- much of the evidence of Roman Aquae Sulis is buried under Georgian Bath;

- lack of primary written sources and apparent contradictions in secondary sources;

- inadequacy of archaeological methods of Victorian times, when much evidence was lost/destroyed;

- incomplete or broken/vandalized remains.

LINKS WITH CITIZENSHIP

DEVELOPING SKILLS OF ENQUIRY AND COMMUNICATION

- Pupils learn how to express, justify and defend personal opinions orally and in writing.

- They research political, social and historical issues and events by analysing information from a variety of sources.

- They contribute to group and class discussions.

DEVELOPING SKILLS OF PARTICIPATION AND RESPONSIBLE ACTION

- Pupils learn to use their imagination to consider other people's experiences throughout history and to think about, express and explain what that might have been like.

- They take part responsibly in school activities.

- They will reflect on the process of participating and recognize that responsible participation yields good results individually and collectively.

CHAPTER 10

MODERN FOREIGN LANGUAGES

Foreign languages provide one of the best opportunities for pupils to explore diversity and cultural difference. The study of language cannot be divorced from an awareness of cultural differences. The challenge for language teachers is to turn this awareness into understanding and acceptance of the value of difference.

In most schools the opportunities for exploring differences other than those just across the Channel in Europe will be limited since French, German and Spanish remain the principal languages taught. Some now teach Japanese and this opens whole new doors. However, with some ingenuity it will be possible to explore other countries too. Large parts of equatorial Africa are Francophone. Most of South America speaks Spanish. It should, therefore, be possible to extend the reading to include texts from wider sources and, through the Internet, make direct contact with cultures very different from our own while at the same time extending language skills.

These lessons are set in particular languages and countries but the ideas could be readily transferred into other countries and other languages.

In this chapter we include the following activities:

- Key Stage 3

    – *A series of two or three lessons using the Internet to prepare for an exchange visit to Germany.*

    – *A series of two or three lessons revising hobbies vocabulary in French.*

- Key Stage 4

    – *Two lessons around German vocabulary for the environment.*

German/citizenship, Key Stage 3
TITLE: Using the Internet to prepare for an exchange visit to Germany

TIME REQUIRED: Two or three lessons plus preparation

RESOURCES REQUIRED: www.webwombat.com can be searched by country and by subject matter for foreign language newspaper articles. The main European Union Web site is at http://europa.eu.int

AIMS AND OBJECTIVES

For citizenship:

- To develop confidence in using foreign Internet Web sites.
- To raise awareness of countries of the European Union.

For German:

- To develop independent reading skills for short texts.
- To raise awareness of school links with the Hanover area.
- To understand authentic information about Hanover.

Introduction

This activity was put together to prepare a group for a foreign-exchange visit to Hanover in Germany. This type of activity could be easily adapted to your school visit with your particular language.

Activities

In a networked ICT room:

- Pupils are given a Web site address and a questionnaire which starts them off on the EXPO 2000 homepage www.expo2000.de The questionnaire encourages them to visit all areas of the homepage. Teachers should create their own questionnaires as appropriate.

- Pupils visit the British page and the European Union page.

- Pupils visit pictures and explanations of sights in Hanover.

Follow up

- Pupils work in small groups to pull together a range of vocabulary they have learnt about Hanover and make a short audio tape on the area.

- Links with Hanover are discussed (in English).

LINKS WITH CITIZENSHIP

KNOWLEDGE AND UNDERSTANDING ABOUT BECOMING INFORMED CITIZENS

- Pupils learn about the role of the European Union and gain an understanding of the world as a global community and the political, economic, environmental and social implications of this.

DEVELOPING SKILLS OF ENQUIRY AND COMMUNICATION

- Pupils learn to think about topical political, social and cultural issues and research them using ICT-based sources.

- They justify orally a personal opinion about such issues.

- They contribute to group and exploratory class discussions.

DEVELOPING SKILLS OF PARTICIPATION AND RESPONSIBLE ACTION

- Pupils learn to use their imagination to consider other people's experiences and to think about, express and explain views that are not their own.

French/citizenship, Key Stage 3
TITLE: Revising hobbies vocabulary

TIME REQUIRED: Two or three lessons plus preparation

RESOURCES REQUIRED: Illustrations and text of the topic to be covered plus a video reinforcing the learning

AIMS AND OBJECTIVES

For citizenship:

- To develop awareness of cultural differences between countries.

For French:

- To read and understand activities.

- To revise hobbies vocabulary.

- To appreciate the range of countries in which French is spoken.

- To produce a personal pie chart of class activities.

Introduction

This was designed for a Year 7 mixed-ability group. Pupils have already been introduced to a range of French-speaking children through video. Vocabulary for a range of hobbies has been introduced and practised. This lesson is easily adapted for other languages.

Activities

- Oral revision of activities and vocabulary around hobbies and pastimes. Use questions and answers and small group/pair work.

- Use any resources available to you that deal with the vocabulary that you wish to revise. In this example, we use *Route Nationale, Book 1*, pages 44–45 (Briggs, Goodman-Stephens and Rogers, 1992), a guided reading through two pie charts. These pages include the following information:

  - *Page 44. A pie chart showing the hobbies/activities most prevalent in Corsica, in percentage terms. This includes such activities as watching television (23 per cent), dance class (5 per cent), swimming (4 per cent), playing tennis (5 per cent), seeing friends (5 per cent) and going to the cinema (3 per cent).*

  - *Page 45. A pie chart showing the hobbies/activities most prevalent in the Ivory Coast, in percentage terms. This includes such activities as watching television (21 per cent), seeing friends (10 per cent), karate (10 per cent) telephoning friends (10 per cent) and playing football (5 per cent).*

- Memory test on the pie charts; turn books over and call out the activities.

- Consider the following questions (in English):

  - *Which pie chart is easier to remember?*

  - *Why do you think there is a difference?*

  - *Which activities are not well represented in the Ivory Coast pie chart? Why?*

- Class survey of pupils' own activities. Results are collected and pupils produce their own pie chart as homework.

Follow up

Use the video from *Route Nationale* showing 'Les Pays Francophones' and some children taking part in hobbies.

KNOWLEDGE AND UNDERSTANDING ABOUT BECOMING INFORMED CITIZENS

- Pupils learn about the world as a global community and the social implications of this as they look at the economic and cultural reasons for diversity.

DEVELOPING SKILLS OF ENQUIRY AND COMMUNICATION

- Pupils learn to think about topical social and cultural issues using different sources of information.

- They contribute to group and exploratory class discussions.

DEVELOPING SKILLS OF PARTICIPATION AND RESPONSIBLE ACTION

- Pupils learn to use their imagination to consider other people's experiences and to discuss the differences between them and their own.

German/citizenship, Key Stage 4
TITLE: Environmental vocabulary

TIME REQUIRED: Two lessons plus preparation

AIMS AND OBJECTIVES

For citizenship:

- To develop awareness of varied approaches to environmental issues.

For German:

- To read a simple questionnaire in German.

- To recognize vocabulary related to the environment.

Introduction

This is designed for a Year 11 lower-ability modular group. Module 4 is entitled 'Young Person in Society'. Pupils are aware 'Environment' is one subsection of this.

Activities

■ Distribute a short questionnaire that has been completed by English, German and Belgian pupils as part of a Comenius project. (Comenius is an EU initiative to foster links between schools in countries of the EU within the Socrates initiative. More detail can be found at www.eurplace.org under Education.)

   – *Ask pupils to read the questions and answers which are in a multiple-choice format to get a sense of what is in there.*

   – *Compare answers from the various countries.*

   – *Establish the major difference on the two environmental questions (Belgian and German pupils are much more active in this area).*

■ *Projekt Deutsch, Book 4* textbook, page 126 (Brien, Brien and Dobson, 1993). Link German phrases to pictures.

   – *Page 126 shows a cartoon style illustration of a German street. The shops/businesses shown are a launderette, a market stall, supermarket, hairdressers, petrol station and an industrial plant. People, various amenities, various methods of transport and animals are portrayed. Some of the activities and amenities are clearly environmentally friendly and others are not; some of the businesses obviously subscribe to recycling and antipollution methods and others do not. Underneath the cartoon is a list of German phrases identifying various aspects. These include such things as smoking, tree planting, leaded petrol and sunbathing.*

■ Write out the phrases in 'positive' and 'negative' columns.

Follow up

- Short follow up in English to establish what the pupils in class do or do not do for the environment.

- Ask pupils to design a poster/leaflet showing what could be done for the environment.

- Get them to discuss in German (in a simple format, owing to language limitations), what could be done for the environment within the school and in the local area.

- Later, allow pupils some time to develop their ideas in English as well as German.

LINKS WITH CITIZENSHIP

KNOWLEDGE AND UNDERSTANDING ABOUT BECOMING INFORMED CITIZENS

- Pupils learn about the rights and responsibilities of people (consumers, employers and employees) in different countries, specifically in relation to environmental issues.

- They learn about the opportunities for individuals and voluntary groups to bring about environmental change.

- They learn about people in other countries of the EU.

DEVELOPING SKILLS OF ENQUIRY AND COMMUNICATION

- Pupils learn to research a topical issue using different sources, including the Internet.

- They learn to express, justify and defend their personal opinion about such issues.

- They contribute to group and exploratory class discussions.

DEVELOPING SKILLS OF PARTICIPATION AND RESPONSIBLE ACTION

- Pupils learn to consider other people's experiences and compare them with their own.

CHAPTER 11

RELIGIOUS EDUCATION OR PHILOSOPHY AND BELIEF

Religious education (RE) is all about questions of values. The key strands of current religious education, spiritual, social and moral development, are directly linked to the aims of citizenship teaching through the exploration of different values and beliefs.

There are many opportunities within the RE or philosophy and belief curriculum to explore the moral foundations for democracy and political activity in the world today. There are also plentiful occasions to investigate the moral dilemmas facing people, politicians and businesses today.

In this chapter we include the following activities:

- Key Stage 3

    – *A series of six lessons designed to examine values, wealth and poverty.*

- Key Stage 4

    – *A double lesson to research and discuss euthanasia.*

    – *A series of 15 one-hour lessons studying Buddhism.*

In *Developing Citizenship in Secondary Schools* by the same authors (Chapter 8) there is a description of a whole-school RE or philosophy and belief day which takes as its theme euthanasia and the right to die debate. Workshops from this chapter can also be adapted for lesson use.

Religious education/citizenship, Key Stage 3
TITLE: Beliefs, wealth and poverty: 'The Trading Game'

TIME REQUIRED: A series of six one hour lessons plus preparation time

RESOURCES REQUIRED: 'The Trading Game' is published by Christian Aid as an educational resource (Christian Aid www.christian-aid.org.uk or PO Box 100, London SE1 7RT). *The Handbook of World Development*, edited by P Stephenson (1982) is another useful resource.

AIMS AND OBJECTIVES

For citizenship and for RE/philosophy and belief:

■ To learn how an economic system can create and maintain differences between developed and developing countries.

■ To understand how the economic development of different communities/countries can be either hindered or benefited.

■ To give pupils the opportunity to reflect on their own views about the extent to which the distribution of wealth and resources within and between societies is fair or unfair.

■ To understand the extent to which wealthy individuals or governments within a society have a moral responsibility or duty to help the poor.

■ To consider an individual's rights concerning use of wealth. Pupils will study how religious beliefs and teachings affect attitudes towards wealth and ways in which religions have responded to the inequalities between rich and poor.

Introduction

This activity describes a series of lessons focusing on the social and moral responsibility strand of citizenship. It is designed to help to inform pupils about the unequal distribution of the world's resources and wealth. The series starts with a classroom game and is followed by several research and discussion sessions. The game can only provide a simple outline of some complex relationships, but it should highlight the way in which the gap between rich and poor/developed and developing is maintained and even widened by a trading system that works in favour of more powerful countries at the expense of weaker nations so that profits are not shared out equally. The main differences are identified through follow-up research on the Brandt Report (*The Handbook of World Development*, edited by P Stephenson, is a good place to start). In addition, time spent focusing on the work of at least one charity organization/development agency will help pupils to understand how improvements can be made to address some of the suffering caused by inequalities in the distribution of wealth.

'The Trading Game'

'The Trading Game' is a comprehensive and exciting game designed to help players understand how trade can affect the prosperity of a country. It is published by Christian Aid as an educational resource. (Christian Aid www.christian-aid.org.uk or PO Box 100, London SE1 7RT). It involves the use of simple resources representing raw materials which can be easily turned into 'manufactured' products in the form of paper shapes. Different groups represent different types of country (eg USA, UK as developed countries, India, Brazil as developing countries and Tanzania, Myanmar (formerly Burma) as underdeveloped countries) with different resource sets in terms of raw materials, tools and finance.

The rules of the game are explained and pupils are divided into groups of four or five. Each group takes the part of a particular country, either developed, developing or underdeveloped. Easily available resources are allocated to groups who then use them to try to trade in order to make money and win the game, with minimal teacher intervention.

Discussion

At the end of the game pupils write a report of their experiences as a participant focusing especially on:

■ what was fair and unfair;

- the attitudes witnessed and experienced by themselves and others;

- how easy or difficult it was to trade with other countries; what deals or alliances took place;

- ways in which the game parallels the real world on a local, national and/or international level.

The reports can be used as the basis for a class discussion of the issues raised.

Development

Later lessons are then devoted to the following activities:

- Carrying out research on the Brandt Report, to examine key terms such as the North–South Divide, between developed and developing countries; to identify important differences between the wealth and resources of countries in the North and South and suggest causes of these differences and the impact on lifestyles. Pupils should present their findings as examples of differences and statistical evidence in a pictorial/illustrative form.

- Using poetry, songs or stories to explore the various attitudes which people may have towards these differences.

- Researching the teachings of one or more world religions about the use of wealth (eg use the story of the Rich Man and Lazarus and Jesus' teaching in the Sermon on the Mount) to introduce a debate on whether the rich bear a moral and social responsibility towards the poor.

- Pupils prepare speeches and questions for a debate (eg use Islamic teaching about gambling to introduce a debate on whether a national lottery should be legal).

- Research religious (and non-religious) responses to the unequal distribution of wealth (eg the work of a development agency such as CAFOD, Christian Aid, or Oxfam or the working and impact of *zakat*, a religious tax, as one of the five pillars of Islam). The Internet is one source of useful information.

Follow up

- Pupils could produce their own decorated poems for display on Treasures of Life (title taken from Jesus' Sermon on the Mount about material and non-material values, Matthew chapter 6 v. 19).

- Pupils are also encouraged to organize and participate in school-based charity initiatives.

- Pupils participate in national initiatives such as Operation Christmas Child providing shoeboxes filled with children's gifts to send to developing countries.

LINKS WITH CITIZENSHIP

KNOWLEDGE AND UNDERSTANDING ABOUT BECOMING INFORMED CITIZENS

- Pupils learn about global inequalities and the effect of trade.

- They learn about the work of religious and non-governmental aid organizations.

DEVELOPING SKILLS OF ENQUIRY AND COMMUNICATION

- Pupils evaluate different viewpoints on the responsibilities of the rich towards the poor.

- They express their opinions both orally and in the form of written speeches or questions.

DEVELOPING SKILLS OF PARTICIPATION AND RESPONSIBLE ACTION

- Pupils participate actively in a game simulating world trade. This gives them an opportunity to learn how the process of trading actually works and, in particular, who wins and who loses.

Religious education/citizenship, Key Stage 4
TITLE: Research and discussion of euthanasia

TIME REQUIRED: A double lesson plus preparation time

RESOURCES REQUIRED: A range of material covering all aspects of the euthanasia debate. Some examples are given below and the Internet can provide useful information and comment.

AIMS AND OBJECTIVES

For citizenship and for RE/philosophy and belief:

■ To research the complex subject of euthanasia.

■ To consider euthanasia from some religious perspectives.

■ To consider euthanasia from the point of view of human rights and the law, in Britain and elsewhere.

■ To reach informed opinions on euthanasia and express them in class discussions.

Introduction

Research the issue of euthanasia, defining key concepts such as voluntary/non-voluntary euthanasia, active and passive euthanasia. Outline the legal perspective comparing approaches in Britain with other countries including the Netherlands. Research some religious perspectives from the tradition of Christianity and/or one other world religion.

Discussion

Through discussion, identify the aspects of religious teachings that have influenced the legal framework. There are then two possible routes forward. Either use poems to stimulate discussion about the right to die; the following three (taken from *Stopping for Death,* edited by Carol Ann Duffy published by Viking (1996) available in paperback) might form a useful collection:

Let me Die a Youngman's Death by Roger McGough;

The Suicides by Janet Frame;

Reincarnation by Sujata Bhatt.

Or, alternatively, break the pupils into groups to discuss the following questions. They should be prepared to present their views back to the whole group in a five-minute informal presentation at the end of the discussion period.

- Is active euthanasia (involving some intervention) better or worse than passive euthanasia (where care and treatment are withdrawn) and why?

- Assisted suicide requires the help of a doctor who provides the means of death. How acceptable is that?

- Should those in a persistent vegetative state (PVS) or prolonged coma have their lives terminated on the grounds that it is no life and their families suffer distress and financial hardship? PVS can persist for many years and recovery is unusual after three months and 'extremely unlikely' after a year.

- Are there any circumstances in which involuntary euthanasia could be acceptable?

- What might prevent euthanasia being made legal?

Extension work

- A formal debate could be held on the motion: 'This house believes that people have the right to die.'

- Pupils could write an essay explaining and justifying their views on euthanasia.

KNOWLEDGE AND UNDERSTANDING ABOUT BECOMING INFORMED CITIZENS

- Pupils learn about the legal and human rights and responsibilities underpinning society.

- They learn about the diversity between countries on controversial moral and social issues.

DEVELOPING SKILLS OF ENQUIRY AND COMMUNICATION

- Pupils learn to research a topical moral and social issue by analysing information from a variety of sources.

- They learn to form and express a personal opinion about a highly contentious moral issue.

DEVELOPING SKILLS OF PARTICIPATION AND RESPONSIBLE ACTION

- Pupils learn to use their imagination to consider other people's experiences and to think about, express, explain and critically evaluate views that are not their own.

- They take part responsibly in group discussion of a difficult moral issue.

Religious education/citizenship, Key Stage 4
TITLE: A study of Buddhism

TIME REQUIRED: This section of work is approximately 15 lessons (each of one hour's duration) and can be used as a piece of coursework with the appropriate board. The coursework details used here are based on requirements from the EDEXCEL Religious Studies syllabus (1478, 1479).

AIMS AND OBJECTIVES

For citizenship, and philosophy and belief:

- To understand Buddhist attitudes to work.

- To understand and be able to use specialist Buddhist terms.

- To show evidence of religious/moral reasoning, typically by reference to another point of view.

- To give a balanced presentation of alternative points of view, including a reasoned account of a personal viewpoint, emphasizing the religious/moral dimension.

Introduction

Pupils need to familiarize themselves with basic Buddhist beliefs. This can be done using a number of methods:

- A visit to a Buddhist monastery, for example, the Amavarati Monastery in Hertfordshire (contact The Venerable Kusalo at Amavarati Buddhist Monastery, Great Gaddesden, Hertfordshire, HP1 3BZ or e-mail: venKusalo@ndirect.co.uk). A worksheet for site work observation is included later. Pupils also require some drawing paper. A number of publications are available at the monastery.

- Research using appropriate texts. Those suggested are:

    - Examining Religions: Moral Issues in Six Religions, *edited by W Owen Cole (1991);*

    - Buddhism for Today, *by Chris Wright (1999).*

- Internet research. An appropriate Web site is http://jbe.la.psu.edu

- Watching the video 'Living Buddhism' from The Clear Vision Trust, a video resource for the new RE syllabus. e-mail clearvision@c-vision.demon.co.uk

Development

Buddhist attitudes to work – essay

Once pupils have a background knowledge of Buddhist beliefs the work to be completed, preferably in an essay form of not more than 1500 words, relates to 'Buddhist attitudes to work'. This essay should be divided into two sections:

1. (a) Show how teaching about Right Livelihood can influence choice of employment.

   (b) Show how teaching about the five pansils can influence choice of employment.

   (c) Explain how some aspects of work in Western societies might be seen by Buddhists to be against their principles.

2. Give your response to the view that 'Everyone has the right to work'. Give reasons for your answer showing that you have considered other points of view.

Research should be undertaken in order to complete the work. The following texts are appropriate. (Useful page numbers are given.)

Buddhism: A New Approach, by Steve Clarke and Mel Thompson (1999) pages 10, 11, 20, 25, 47, 69, 70, 72, 76 and the glossary.

The Buddhist Experience, by Mel Thompson (1998) pages 10, 11, 20, 21, 31, 34, 35 and the glossary.

Guidelines for completing the essay are in the 'Extension' section starting on page 149.

Questions about Buddhism and work

Ask pupils to answer all the questions below:

1. Look up and explain these words as clearly and in as much detail as you can: *metta*; *karuna*; *vipassana*.

2. The Fifth Step of the Eightfold path is Right Livelihood. Explain in detail what Buddhists mean by 'Right Livelihood'.

3. What is the difference between employment and work? Use examples to explain your answer.

4. Make a list of jobs or work which you think would be suitable for a Buddhist. Give reasons for each of your choices.

5. Make a list of jobs or work which you think would be unsuitable for a Buddhist. Give reasons for each of your choices.

6. Choose one job from your list for Question 3 and show how this job would enable a Buddhist to develop *metta* (loving kindness) and *karuna* (compassion).

7. Describe and explain one job that would enable a Buddhist to have a positive effect on the environment.

8. Describe and explain one job that would enable a Buddhist to keep a sense of peace that Buddhism seeks to offer.

9. Explain, with reference to Buddhist teachings, what a Buddhist's attitude might be to each of the following: pay, employers, employees, customers. Remember to use specialist Buddhist terms when you can.

10. What do Buddhists mean when they talk about 'skilful means'?

11. Invent and describe briefly a problem situation which might arise in the workplace as a result of: selfishness, greed, exploitation of workers (taking advantage of others), exploitation of animals, laziness or dishonesty.

Show how Buddhist teachings might be applied to each of these situations. Use specialist terms where you can.

Further development work

■ Invite representatives from 'Evolution' to make a presentation/ talk to pupils; Evolution is part of the 'Friends of the Western Buddhist Order'. This is an organization that sees business in terms of a fellowship rather than in terms of greed, power, etc.

- Pupils can be encouraged to look at Web sites relating to forestry, garden centres, etc.

- Pupils might also like to look at *Working in the Right Spirit: The Application of Buddhist Right Livelihood in the Friends of the Western Buddhist Order*, by Martin Baumann (University of Hanover, Germany) martin.baumann@HRZ.Uni-Bielefeld.de

Extension

Guidelines for completing the Buddhist attitudes to work essay

Section 1(a)

Ask pupils to draft a piece on Buddhist attitudes to work to form Part 1 (a) (see page 147) of their essays. In this piece they should show how teaching about Right Livelihood can influence choice of employment. In order to do this they will need to consider the following questions:

- What is the Buddhist teaching about Right Livelihood?

- Where is the teaching to be found?

- How does it relate to the Eightfold Path? Which step of the Eightfold Path is it? Is it part of the Way of Wisdom or the Way of Morality or the Way of Meditation?

- How does teaching about Right Livelihood fit in with other aspects of Buddhist beliefs? For example:

    – *the Four Noble Truths;*

    – *the Three Marks of Existence* (annica, anatta, dukkha*);*

    – *the Middle Way;*

    – metta *(loving kindness);*

    – karuna *(compassion);*

    – *enlightenment;*

    – karma/samsara *and the wheel of life;*

– skilful and unskilful means.

Once pupils are familiar with Buddhist beliefs they should think about how these beliefs would influence choice of employment. They should think about:

- the nature of the work (what types of jobs/occupations would be considered appropriate/inappropriate);

- the work environment; attitudes to and treatment of staff and conditions of employment;

- the goal of the employment, eg to make money or to help others;

- the effect of the work on spiritual development, the environment, the local community and the wider national/international community.

Why do these things matter to Buddhists?

Are there examples of Buddhists at work that pupils could refer to, eg the shops of the Evolution organization? Pupils can be encouraged to use other sources of information from their own independent research, eg CD ROM, interviews with Buddhist monks during the visit to the monastery, magazine articles, the video or appropriate texts.

Once Section 1(a) has been completed, Section 1(b) can be started.

Section 1(b)

- Pupils to look back at their notes on the Five Precepts. They are relevant to this section. It might also be useful to show Programme 3 *The Five Precepts in Practice* section from 'Living Buddhism', a video resource for the new RE syllabus. e-mail clearvision@c-vision.demon.co.uk

- What are the Five Precepts? Why do Buddhists hold certain moral beliefs? How do the precepts fit in with other Buddhist beliefs and teachings?

- Think about how each one of the precepts might affect a Buddhist at work. Again pupils might like to think along the lines of the nature of the work, the work environment, the goal of the work and the effect of the work on self, others, community, environment.

■ Think of some really good examples to illustrate how Buddhists might put the Five Precepts into practice at work. Are there any articles from the media that pupils could use to show what a Buddhist would consider to be good or bad? For example, work of charity organizations to relieve suffering where there have been natural disasters.

Once Section 1(b) has been completed, pupils need to address Section 1(c).

Section 1(c)

■ In order to do this, pupils should be encouraged to brainstorm various aspects of work in Western society for example:

– *aims of work: profit-making/wealth/capitalism;*

– *hierarchies at work: relationships between employers/employees;*

– *working environment: conditions/facilities;*

– *pressures in the workplace: meeting deadlines;*

– *causes of stress: hours of work workload/demands.*

Relate the above to specific examples of employment, eg industrial work, advertising, journalism, law, retail industry, farming, caring professions.

■ Ensure pupils understand key Buddhist principles:

– *goal of enlightenment;*

– *suffering caused by Craving/Three Poisons: hatred, greed, ignorance;*

– *right action;*

– *right speech;*

– meeta;

– karuna;

– *meditation: training and control of the mind,* smaths *and* vipassana *meditation;*

– *peace;*

– *'Middle Way' in between extremes.*

- Ask pupils to look at how and why any points in the first list above might go against Buddhist principles listed in the second, eg greed as a poison (in the second list) might be linked with profit making (in the first). See how many points pupils can link together from each list.

Section 2

- Remind pupils of the statement 'Everyone has the right to work'. Do you agree? Give reasons for your answer showing that you have considered alternative views. (Include a Buddhist point of view.)

- Look at the key words in the question. Advise the pupils to think about what these words might mean and jot their ideas down: 'everyone'; 'right'; 'work'.

- Pupils to decide whether they agree with the statement. Pupils to think of evidence or examples which could be used to *support* or *oppose* the statement 'Everyone has the right to work' and list these in two columns.

- How might a Buddhist respond to this statement? Pupils to jot down any beliefs they may have come across which could be applied to this question.

- Pupils should be encouraged to identify any moral issues which might be relevant to this question, eg the issues of discrimination and levels of responsibility needed for some jobs, the importance of skills and qualifications.

- Pupils should look at all the evidence and arguments they have gathered. The different views need to be weighed up to show which arguments are strong and which are weak. The final personal view of the pupil must be stated; it is possible to remain undecided as long as there is a rationale for this.

- Finally, pupils should write up the complete essay in a clear and organized style.

VISIT TO A BUDDHIST MONASTERY – WORKSHEET

1.   What evidence is there that the vihara is a place of:

   (a) devotion?
   (b) meditation?
   (c) study?

_____

_____

_____

_____

_____

_____

2.   Draw (on the paper provided) and describe three artefacts which may be found in a
     Buddhist shrine. How are each of these used in worship?

_____

_____

_____

_____

_____

_____

_____

3.   Outline a daily timetable for a monk.

_____

_____

_____

_____

_____

4.   List any techniques used in Buddhist meditation. Describe and explain at least one particular type or example of a meditation which a monk might use.

_____

_____

_____

_____

5.   How does the way in which food is provided for the monk's daily meal help a monk?

_____

_____

_____

_____

6. What forms of work might a Buddhist undertake at this monastery? Give details of at least one example.

_____

_____

_____

_____

7. What words sum up the atmosphere of the monastery for you?

_____

_____

_____

_____

8. How might the life of a monk at the monastery help a Buddhist to reach enlightenment?

_____

_____

_____

_____

_____

KNOWLEDGE AND UNDERSTANDING ABOUT BECOMING INFORMED CITIZENS

- Pupils learn about the moral and human rights underpinning society and how they relate to citizens.

- They learn about the origins and implications of some diverse religious identities in the United Kingdom and the need for mutual respect and understanding.

- They learn about how the economy functions, including the role of business.

- They learn about the importance of a free press and the media's role in society, including the Internet, in providing information and affecting opinion.

- They learn about the opportunities for individuals and voluntary groups to bring about social change.

- They learn about the rights and responsibilities of consumers, employers and employees.

- The learn about the wider issues and challenges of global interdependence and responsibility.

DEVELOPING SKILLS OF ENQUIRY AND DEBATE

- Pupils learn to research a topical moral or social issue by analysing information from different sources, including ICT-based sources.

- They justify orally and in writing a personal opinion about such issues.

- They contribute to group and exploratory class discussions.

DEVELOPING SKILLS OF PARTICIPATION AND RESPONSIBLE ACTION

- Pupils learn to use their imagination to consider other people's experiences and to think about, express and explain views that are not their own.

- They learn to negotiate, decide and take part responsibly in school.

- They learn to reflect on the process of participating.

CHAPTER 12

ART AND MUSIC

Art and Music are both core elements of the curriculum. At first sight it might seem difficult to make clear links between the teaching of these subjects and citizenship. However, closer examination will reveal that there are clear opportunities to learn about citizenship. For instance, the internal reflection on how to represent or depict a theme or issue and the intellectual engagement that participation in art brings are clearly ways of thinking and behaving that must underpin learning about citizenship. It becomes clear that the practice of art in all its forms encourages the skills of making personal judgements and formulating opinion and of communicating those judgements and opinions to others.

More directly there are obvious opportunities for citizenship learning around the subject matter of art. The story being depicted, the scene displayed, the situation experienced can all be the starting point for discussions about values, rights and the opinions of other diverse groups.

This chapter describes the following activities:

Art

- Key Stage 3

    - *A course of lessons, designed to last up to a term, using masks to explore shape, form and different cultural expression.*

- Key Stage 4

    - *A course of lessons, spread over a term or more, to explore the work of Beryl Cook. The work is used to explore regional and cultural diversity.*

Music

■ Key Stage 3

  – *One lesson using the blues idiom as a means of exploring slavery and European involvement in it.*

■ Key Stage 4

  – *A double lesson on twentieth-century composition and exploring the place of music politically and in society.*

Art/citizenship, Key Stage 3
TITLE: Three-dimensional card sculpture

TIME REQUIRED: A course of lessons designed to last for up to a term

RESOURCES REQUIRED: Examples of masks from a variety of sources; these could include photographs, pictures, diagrams, theatrical masks, etc

AIMS AND OBJECTIVES

For citizenship:

■ To investigate art, craft and design in a variety of styles from a range of historical, social and cultural contexts.

■ To be aware of the diversity of religious and ethnic identities in the UK and the need for mutual respect and understanding.

For art:

■ To introduce pupils to proportion, measurement and the positioning of features in the human face.

■ To explore ideas and develop designs which will translate to card sculpture.

■ To encourage imaginative and creative use of materials.

Introduction

■ Discuss the proportions of the human head; make use of visual materials.

■ Demonstrate techniques of measuring features, proportions, etc.

■ Pupils work in pairs and use each other as models to identify features of the face and head.

Self-portrait study

Pupils prepare a linear self-portrait study in pencil. Emphasize proportion and the positioning and detail of features.

Introduction of the concept of 'mask'

■ Look at and discuss a range of non-European masks. Extract features and detail relevant ideas from visual examples.

■ Pupils develop personal mask designs.

Development: Extended assignment

This work can be done in class or as a homework project.

■ Discuss the use of masks in religious and ethnic groups in the UK, eg in the Chinese New Year dragon dance and carnival celebrations.

■ Ask pupils to identify an area of study and research information from a variety of sources, eg Encarta, the Internet, art books, gallery or museum guides, postcards, historical/cultural source books, etc.

■ Ask pupils to comment on how the use of masks and performances make a positive impact on society.

Creating 3D card sculptures

■ Discuss approach and techniques and demonstrate possibilities.

■ Pupils develop their mask designs with cut card shapes.

■ Pupils explore cutting, folding, assembling, colour, decorative elements and character.

LINKS WITH CITIZENSHIP

KNOWLEDGE AND UNDERSTANDING ABOUT BECOMING INFORMED CITIZENS

■ Pupils learn about the diversity of national, regional, religious and ethnic identities in the UK and elsewhere.

DEVELOPING SKILLS OF ENQUIRY AND COMMUNICATION

■ Pupils learn to think about social and cultural issues and events using information from different sources, including the Internet.

■ They express and justify their personal opinions about such issues or events.

■ They contribute to exploratory class discussions.

DEVELOPING SKILLS OF PARTICIPATION AND RESPONSIBLE ACTION

■ Pupils learn to use their imagination to consider other people's experiences and to think about and compare these experiences with their own.

Art/citizenship, Key Stage 4
TITLE: 'A Slice of Life', the paintings of Beryl Cook

TIME REQUIRED: This piece of work is designed to last over one to one-and-a-half terms

RESOURCES REQUIRED: Reproductions of the work of Beryl Cook. Material containing illustrations of people from diverse ethnic, religious and cultural backgrounds from books, magazines, postcards, computer programs, etc.

AIMS AND OBJECTIVES

For citizenship:

■ To study work which includes cultural, religious and ethnic diversity in order to understand that diversity and the need for mutual respect and understanding.

For art:

■ To introduce pupils to proportion and measurement when drawing the human figure.

■ To explore the possibilities of poses and groupings of figures to suggest dynamic interrelationships.

■ To explore and become familiar with the work of Beryl Cook and to demonstrate understanding of her compositional and stylistic devices.

Introduction

■ Discuss proportions of the human figure.

■ Discuss how to simplify the human body into basic shapes.

■ Discuss how the visual material can be used to aid the work.

■ Demonstrate techniques of drawing the figure.

Figure drawings

Explore the use of figure drawings using:

- linear studies using pencil; emphasize proportions;

- experiment with groupings of figures and explore interactions between the figures.

Introduction to the work of Beryl Cook

- Look at a range of examples of Beryl Cook's work.

- Discuss in terms of content, atmosphere, colour, interaction, humour, style, composition, depth, dynamism, etc.

- Pupils make notes and sketches to illustrate the above issues.

Extended assignment

To research, develop and evaluate a composition that explores the diversity of religious, cultural and ethnic identities within the UK.

- Select a setting for 'A Slice of Life', eg a local carnival, a club, a sport venue, public transport, shops, a park or public space, etc and then build up a bank of appropriate visual resources including drawings and photographs.

- Experiment with composition to convey atmosphere. Adapt and refine ideas.

- Produce a final piece that makes use of the compositional and stylistic devices employed by Beryl Cook.

- Evaluate the project.

LINKS WITH CITIZENSHIP

KNOWLEDGE AND UNDERSTANDING ABOUT BECOMING INFORMED CITIZENS

- Pupils learn about the origins and implications of the diverse national, regional, religious and ethnic identities in the United Kingdom and the need for mutual respect and understanding.

DEVELOPING SKILLS OF ENQUIRY AND COMMUNICATION

- Pupils learn to research a topical political, social or cultural issue using information from different sources including ICT based sources.

- They contribute to group and exploratory class discussions.

DEVELOPING SKILLS OF PARTICIPATION AND RESPONSIBLE ACTION

- Pupils learn to use their imagination to consider other people's experiences and to think about and express views that are not their own.

Music/citizenship, Key Stage 3
TITLE: Chords and Blues

TIME REQUIRED: Single lesson plus preparation

AIMS AND OBJECTIVES

For citizenship:

- To raise awareness of cultural differences and the impact of history on communities.

For music:

- To enable pupils to recognise and use simple chords of III, IV and V through the study of blues music, in particular the 12-bar blues.

- To introduce blues music and its history. Pupils should gain an awareness of the historical development of this music and recognise its basic sound.

Introduction

1. Set seats out in a semicircle around the board.

2. Play an example of blues music as the class enter the room. Once pupils are settled ask them to note down any words, phrases or facts that are suggested to them by what they hear; these might be instruments, the words or the music, historical context, social issues, etc.

3. Go through answers in a brainstorming session putting relevant points on the board. Any irrelevant comments should be acknowledged but omitted. Only fill in the central legend 'BLUES' if it is suggested, otherwise add this at the end.

4. Explain that blues is to be the lesson topic.

Musical exercise

- Pupils stand in a semicircle and the teacher leads a *'call* and *echo'*.

- This activity flows into *'call* and *response'*.

- Pupils are invited to lead *'call* and *response'*.

- The teacher finishes with *'call* and *echo'* to regain control.

Development

- With pupils back in their seats the teacher draws a map of the Atlantic circle on the board (pupils should be provided with a printed copy to stick in their books).

- Explain how Europe, as a small and habitable area, developed more quickly than the massive continent of Africa. Europeans began to explore and travel; illustrate travel with arrows on the map.

- Enslaved black Africans were taken to Europe and the New World of America.

- As slaves, forced to work on the land, the Africans sang songs to help them get through the day. These were repetitive so that they could work with a rhythm. Usually the songs were led by one person as a call and response or call and echo, like the songs sung earlier in the lesson.

- Finish the lesson by singing the songs through once more.

LINKS WITH CITIZENSHIP

KNOWLEDGE AND UNDERSTANDING ABOUT BECOMING INFORMED CITIZENS

- Pupils become aware of some of the basic issues around slavery and human rights.
- They become aware of prejudice and their own stereotyping through an examination of their attitudes/response to the music.

DEVELOPING SKILLS OF ENQUIRY AND COMMUNICATION

- Pupils learn to form, express and justify opinions about both the music and slavery.

Music/citizenship, Key Stage 4
TITLE: Twentieth-century composition

TIME REQUIRED: A double lesson plus preparation

AIMS AND OBJECTIVES

For citizenship:

- To recognize some of the effects and characteristics of diversity in society.

- To gain understanding of the role of government regarding the arts.

For music:

- To enable pupils to compose using a variety of techniques developed in the twentieth century and to understand why they developed when they did.

- To focus specifically on 12-tone composition and the second Viennese school. Pupils will be able to compose a short piece for two or three instruments using this method.

Activity

- As the class enter have a piece of Schoenberg's 12-tone music playing.

- Leave the piece playing quietly while the register is taken. This will enable pupils to begin forming opinions about it. Ask pupils to write down in their books any thoughts, feelings or ideas as well as factual speculation, such as instrumentation, possible period of composition, etc.

- Canvas results and note them all on the board.

- Write a heading 'Serialism' on the board and, using a time line through the historical periods of music, describe how the strict rules of harmony gradually became less and less relevant until, at the beginning of the twentieth century, there were none left.

- Pose the question: 'Where do you go if there are no rules left to be broken?'

- Introduce Schoenberg and his new ideas of no tonality at all.

- Give pupils a work sheet showing the basic rules of serialism and work through each rule.

- Pupils are given a specified tone row. Individually, they must give it rhythm and turn it into a piece of solo music.

- Hear each pupil's piece and discuss. In particular, is there a melody? How could the music develop? Introduce 'retrograde' and 'inversion'.

- Ask pupils to find the retrograde and inversion of the specified tone row.

- Ask pupils to compose their own tone row using each of the 12 notes only once. They must find all forms of their tone row.

- Listen to each piece and discuss. Which ones work best and why?

- In groups of three or four, combine the tone rows to create texture. Work towards performance of each piece at the end of the lesson.

Discussion

Discuss the popularity or otherwise of this form of music. Should such music be funded from the public purse? There is the claim that avant-garde music attracts funding because it is 'intellectual' and new, while more popular genres may receive no funding at all. But if there is no change, can progress occur?

This will lead the discussion into the much wider field of funding for the arts in general. Is funding for opera élitist? Why do some theatre companies attract a subsidy and others not? Should such funding be left to lottery grants?

Relate these discussions to topical projects in your area.

LINKS WITH CITIZENSHIP

KNOWLEDGE AND UNDERSTANDING ABOUT BECOMING INFORMED CITIZENS

- Pupils learn about the rights of different people to have diverse opinions and tastes. Tolerance is essential for these diverse views to co-exist peacefully.

- They learn about the role of government in funding of the arts and in particular issues around the funding of the new or intellectual and under-funding of 'popular' music.

DEVELOPING SKILLS OF ENQUIRY AND COMMUNICATION

- Pupils learn to express their opinions and allow others the right to express theirs.

- They take part in class discussions.

CHAPTER 13

DRAMA

Drama is an extremely powerful medium for the teaching of citizenship. In Chapter 3 we set out, in some detail, ways that drama can be used in any subject lesson to promote learning about citizenship. In this chapter we take some specific drama lessons and show how the teaching of drama and citizenship can profitably go hand in hand.

The nature of the work chosen is the key. Learning about drama can be achieved through a huge variety of situations that it is possible to ask pupils to play and address. The issues of democracy, human rights and diversity (among others), the core of the citizenship curriculum, make ideal subjects and can raise all the feelings and relationship issues that make for good drama. The two curricula sit well together.

As in other chapters, we set out at the end of each lesson or series of lessons those elements of citizenship – Links with Citizenship – that we believe are covered within the material given. In the case of drama that is more difficult. It is worth making the point that the subject nature of the scenario(s) chosen for drama work will determine, to a large extent, the learning that it is possible to achieve. If, for example, one of the scenarios was about drugs and drug offenders a wide range of issues could emerge from discussion and be used by the member of staff as a teaching aid. The links we describe are, therefore, really only indicative. The limit is only the imagination of the teacher and, of course, of the pupils involved.

In this chapter we include the following activities:

- Key Stage 3

    - *A series of three to six double lessons based around the employees in a factory.*

- Key Stage 4

– A series of lessons to prepare a performance around the theme 'Crime is Complicated'. Within this course are a couple of lessons which could be used separately: one explores character status and the other is a repetition exercise demonstrating the value of acting with others rather than in isolation.

Drama/citizenship, Key Stage 3
TITLE: Lloyd's Leisure Products

TIME REQUIRED: A series of three to six double lessons plus preparation

AIMS AND OBJECTIVES

For citizenship:

- To introduce the pupils to both physical and realistic theatre and to learn to empathize with the views and opinions of others.

- To highlight how theatre can be used to simulate conflict and its resolution.

- To encourage pupils to make democratic decisions in group work.

For drama:

- To give experience of both small group and paired improvisation.

- To emphasize the importance of thorough rehearsal.

- To demonstrate the techniques of role playing.

- To develop evaluative skills.

- To encourage pupils to use their imaginations to create and sustain an appropriate character.

■ To illustrate how movement, voice and eye contact can be used to convey a range of emotions.

Lesson 1

Introduction

The teacher explains that a new factory is opening in the seaside town of Bashton-on-Sea. The factory is called Lloyd's Leisure Products and makes beach and sports equipment. Visual aids of appropriate buildings/locations could be used.

Discussion

The teacher asks for specific examples of the types of equipment the factory might make. This could be done by a brainstorm. The teacher demonstrates the human machine by using five volunteers to represent the different elements of the manufacturing process. The movement should be stylized and show changes in height, size and speed. Each stage of the machine should have a clear noise and action which lasts the same length of time as the other steps so that once pupil one has completed his or her 'job' the product can be passed down the conveyor belt to pupil two. Once this has been done, pupil one can repeat the first action.

Development

In groups of five, the pupils choose a different object that the factory makes, eg tennis rackets, beach balls, etc. Pupils work on the sound effects for the machine to make the required object(s). After five to ten minutes rehearsal each group demonstrates their machine.

■ The teacher explains that a job advert has appeared in the local press. Since it is now autumn and all of the summer holiday trade has finished, unemployment is running high and everyone is desperate for a job. The teacher explains that the pupils need to imagine they are aged 16–18 and that they have just left school and need full-time employment. Since this is too good an opportunity to miss, everyone applies for a job and, coincidentally, they are all invited to interview. The teacher takes the role of Martin(e) Lloyd, the Managing Director (MD), welcomes everyone to Lloyds Leisure Products, wishes them the best of luck and explains that they will demonstrate the interview procedure and asks for a volunteer. Although the role is pompous and slightly patronizing the character must also appear to be caring.

- Basic questions are asked in this role play about why the applicant wants the job, what experience he or she has and what suggestions they may have for improving the factory in any way. After demonstrating the interview the teacher comes out of role and explains that it is now the turn of the pupils.

- In pairs the pupils decide who is going to be the MD and who is going to be the interviewee. Pupils who are to play the MD are encouraged to adopt appropriate characteristics. After a couple of minutes of improvised drama, the pupils in each pair swap roles, so that they have the opportunity to play different characters.

- Bring the class back together in a circle. The teacher, back in role as the MD, congratulates them on getting the job and explains to them that they must let the MD know if they have any problems. Interviewees are also warned that the factory works on trust and if any employee talks to the press about anything that happens in the factory they will be sacked and prosecuted.

Conclusion

Out of role, the teacher asks the pupils about their initial impressions of the MD. Can he or she be trusted?

Lesson 2

Introduction

The teacher explains that, following an excellent advertising campaign, sales have gone through the roof. This does mean that the workers will be paid more but they will also have to work six days a week and all holidays will have to be cancelled. In addition, they are starting to have some of the teething problems which might be expected in a new factory.

Discussion

The teacher asks the class to consider what these teething problems might be. This could be done by brainstorming. Pupils may suggest a leaking roof, blocked toilets, canteen closed by health inspectors, always working on the same machine, falling motivation as the novelty wears off, etc.

Development

Working in pairs, pupil A is the MD and B is a factory worker. The As and Bs are sent to separate sides of the room so that different instructions can be given to each half of the class.

- The Bs must be very nervous about talking to the MD of the company. They need to think about how this might show through in their movement, voice and eye contact.

- The As must be very abrupt and unhelpful. Every time a problem is raised they must come up with a list of excuses explaining why it exists and why it is impossible to do anything about it. It is important that As are as devious as possible. Pupils improvise the scene for five minutes.

- The teacher divides the class back into two halves of As and Bs and gives some new instructions.

- This time A is the factory worker. They have realized that being polite and respectful has got them nowhere so this time they should be a lot more demanding. They should be angry and disappointed, which should be revealed in their vocal tone, but they should note that there should be no physical contact.

- B is the MD and must be as kind and understanding as possible. If A is upset she or he should be offered a cup of tea or even a chocolate biscuit. Once again this scene should be improvised for five minutes.

- The teacher then allows a short time for the pupils to select which scenario they are happier with and polish it to performance standard. Some of the pairs perform.

Conclusion

Discussion to identify which of the scenes performed were most effective and why. How could they be improved? What do we now know about the MD? Why do we think he or she is so evasive?

Lesson 3

Introduction

The teacher begins by saying that this morning at work a note was discovered by factory workers in their lockers. It read 'This company is polluting the environment. It is pumping tonnes of hazardous waste into the river. If you want to find out more come to Bashton Village Hall at 7 pm.'

Discussion

Class discusses issues including 'How would you react to this if you were a factory worker? Who might have sent the letter? What did the MD say would happen if you were found talking to people outside of the factory about what goes on inside?'

Development

Working in pairs. It is the lunch break and you want to find out if your friend received a note. What might you say? Can you trust your friend? How can you find out if they got a note without directly asking the question? Improvise a scene in the re-opened cafeteria about the anonymous note. The issue needs to be raised subtly, perhaps by talking about something else/trivial first.

Meanwhile the teacher, back in role as MD, is walking around the canteen, a normal routine. When pairs discussing the letter are approached they must change their topic of conversation quickly to prevent suspicion.

- All pairs should improvise at the same time as the MD patrols the room.

- After five minutes the whole class is brought together and a few of the improvised scenes are performed.

- The teacher explains that as a group of workers they need to make a democratic decision – should they or should they not attend the meeting? Pupils vote. (It is worth noting that in our experience a class has never voted not to go to the secret meeting but they do feel empowered by choosing their own fate!).

- The teacher explains that they need to imagine they are in the village hall. It is 7.10 pm. They are just about to leave when a person arrives. This is the teacher playing a former employee. This person is very evasive, refuses to give a name and, although prepared to answer some of the questions put by the group, is quietly spoken and extremely nervous.

- The teacher, as the former employee, leaves a key to a room in the basement of the factory saying there is toxic waste there. Workers are asked to collect a sample but insist that they must all agree to do so as the risk is so great. The group votes on whether or not to collect a sample. (The vote has always been in favour of doing this.)

- The teacher asks the pupils to sit in a circle to act as the walls of the basement where the toxic waste is treated, leaving a gap for the door.

■ A volunteer is selected for each attempt at collecting a sample. At each attempt, more and more problems are identified by the teacher and suggestions need to be made about how to overcome them before the next attempt is made.

■ The teacher will need to find reasons to dismiss the ideas which do not follow the basic structure. Although it appears very complicated, with a little preparation it runs very smoothly. The attempts at collecting the sample usually go as follows:

1. *One person walks straight into the room to grab a sample. The teacher explains the door shuts behind them and there is no lock on the inside. They are trapped, discovered by security the following day and sacked.*

2. *Two people go down to the basement. One holds the door, the other collects the sample. The teacher in the role of the MD walks down to the basement and discovers the person holding the door and tells them to let go. The person inside is trapped, etc.*

3. *One person goes to distract the MD while the other collects the sample. The MD leaves the office in time to glimpse the person with the sample and interrogates the decoy and demands to know the name of accomplices. The decoy is offered a better job and pay rise. The decoy will need to decide between promotion and the friendship of other employees. If the pupil decides to 'name names' the MD sacks him or her anyway explaining that the company does not want employees who turn their backs on their friends. However, the sample has escaped.*

Conclusion

Discuss the dilemma that faced the employee. What issues might make his or her situation even harder? Perhaps he or she is in debt or has a young family to support.

Further development

Future lessons could involve a television news report on events, interviewing key people involved in the saga and other experts who may wish to comment on events.

LINKS WITH CITIZENSHIP

KNOWLEDGE AND UNDERSTANDING ABOUT BECOMING INFORMED CITIZENS

- Pupils learn about the legal and human rights and responsibilities underpinning society and particularly those around employment.

- They learn the importance of a democratic approach, election systems and the significance of voting.

- They learn about the importance of resolving conflict fairly.

DEVELOPING SKILLS OF ENQUIRY AND DEBATE

- Pupils learn to think about topical political, cultural and social issues, using a variety of sources.

- They form, express and justify personal opinions about such issues.

- They contribute to group and exploratory class discussions.

DEVELOPING SKILLS OF PARTICIPATION AND RESPONSIBLE ACTION

- Pupils learn to use their imagination to consider other people's experiences and to think about, express and explain views that are not their own.

- They learn to negotiate, decide and take part responsibly in both school- and community-based (even if fictional) activities.

- They reflect on the process of participating.

Drama/citizenship, Key Stage 4
TITLE: Crime is complicated

TIME REQUIRED: One single and one double lesson a week for seven weeks, plus preparation, and a performance in week eight. This intensive course could be adapted to fit another timetable.

AIMS AND OBJECTIVES

For citizenship:

- To raise awareness of the many factors that contribute to criminal behaviour.

- To consider issues around the effectiveness of the judicial system and punishment of crime.

For drama:

- To devise a show on the theme of 'Crime is Complicated'.

- To practise a wide range of dramatic techniques and assess their relative effectiveness for different purposes.

Introduction

Pupils consider issues of criminality through the use of drama. They choose issues that must impose dilemmas on the characters: a drug user steals from his family to supply his habit; a gang of vandals targets the shop of a relative of one of them; a young person uses his parents' credit cards, forging signatures in so doing; a young family with heavy debts and rent to pay start shoplifting to feed themselves; a policeman in financial difficulty starts taking bribes from offenders, etc.

Lesson 1: Week 1. Introduction and improvisation

1. The theme of 'Crime is Complicated' is introduced.

2. Pupils are divided into groups for improvisation; five-minutes rehearsal and short performance. They choose their own subject and devise and create their own piece of drama. Advise them that they should not devise a great piece of mayhem, violence and murder but should concentrate instead on moral issues and conflicts.

3. Feedback is given on what was illustrated successfully/ unsuccessfully. Pupils are advised to concentrate on tension in the story and on maintaining role.

4. New improvisations, with tension and maintenance of roles, eg thief may not just be evil but may have a poor family, vandals choose the shop belonging to the uncle of one of them to wreck.

5. Homework: each pupil writes up a journal of what they did and what they learnt.

Lessons 2/3: Week 1

1. In groups, using sugar paper, 15 minutes to brainstorm four scenes around the theme of 'Crime is Complicated'.

2. Give feedback on what *kinds* of issues are available. What tensions are there operating in your scenes/plays? Offer constructive advice on how to improve.

3. Beginnings: 10 minutes to improvise Scene I. Perform some, then look at tension, staying in role and creating interest in an opening scene.

4. Model: how can you create interest in a beginning? Use of music, movement, sound, surprise, flashback.

5. Either take one group, and replay their scene but with alternative openings to catch interest, or work in small groups on ideas for new openings and begin to rehearse. The teacher

checks that all are under way. Possibly have some of the scenes performed.

6. Homework: plan possible alternatives for openings.

Lesson 4: Week 2. Reflection

1. Finalize four to six scenes on sugar paper. Check that there is tension.

2. Question: What else is needed? Characters will be dealt with later but look for variety to maintain interest.

3. Model: the teacher runs through a narrative-led play with plenty of action but no reflection of what is happening, just a sequence of events.

4. Handout: Table 13.1. Discuss ways to break up the flow of narrative, allowing you to look at things in different ways. Suggest that groups can either replace some scenes with tableaux, flashbacks, etc or insert them between current scenes, try it in rehearsal and remain flexible.

5. Model: take one group and find a moment to freeze the action, then demonstrate how one character can step out and explain how they feel or how a narrator can introduce other frozen characters.

6. Rehearse freezes and other techniques.

7. Homework: stick Table 13.1 in drama journal and write up.

Lessons 5/6: Week 2

Warn that time is at a premium and that from now on two scenes need to be improvised in each double lesson. Groups should have a clear idea of where they are going; polishing comes later.

1. Ten minutes to finalize understanding of the opening scene. Rehearse.

Table 13.1 Have you ever thought of using ... ?

Monologues Monologues are a good way of giving the audience an insight into a character's mind. However, be careful because they can become repetitive if they are used too often. Try tackling monologues from unusual angles, eg telephone conversations, letter writing, a prayer, a confession or even try two conflicting monologues together.

Poetry Excerpts from poetry can help to develop a mood or situation allowing the audience time to listen to words rather than following action.

Freezes or tableaux These are good to use at the beginning, middle or end of scenes to emphasize the action. They can also be used to symbolize photographs or even to highlight the difference between two states, eg good and evil, dream/nightmare and reality.

Dreams or nightmares Once again, this allows you to break away from naturalistic action. Both of these allow you to develop and exaggerate characters and to experiment with unusual movement and voice work.

Flashback/flash forward Scenes can sometimes become boring if they follow a natural time order. Occasionally, it is useful to use either of these devices to give a hint at past or future action.

Speeches or news headlines These can be real or fictional. They help to give the audience an idea of what effect the event has had on the outside world

Dance/choreographed movement Movement is necessary in all pieces of drama, albeit in quite a basic form. Dance can be used to express the emotion in a particular scene or the relationships between characters. Choreographed movement in the form of mechanized or animalistic motion can be used to break up the naturalistic nature of a scene. It is worth experimenting with the repetition and/or exaggeration of these movements.

Mimes or pauses There is always a tendency to talk too much during improvisational work. Dramatic pauses can allow the audience to 'zoom in' on the smallest of movements. Similarly, you can use short scenes with conversations to contrast with scenes with no dialogue in the previous or following scene, eg a scene with friends at a party is followed by a scene showing another friend who missed the party because they had to baby-sit for their little brother.

Music Music can be used to create mood and atmosphere before, during or after the action. Comic and surreal effects can be created by juxtaposing opposites, eg an argument with comic music.

Remember that in each of your improvisations you should be showing a variety of skills. Please experiment with all of the above but remember you should also try to vary pace, volume, emotion, movement, staging and relationship with the audience.

2. Move on to Scene II. Rehearse, remembering to use tension, techniques and maintaining role.

3. Quickly move on to Scene III. Allow about 10 minutes for one group to perform what they have prepared and for the class to analyse and reflect.

4. Suggest that groups may wish to find extra time during lunch break or after school to practise and perfect what they have done. The idea is to get the groups working to a tight schedule but, if this becomes difficult, this double lesson may be used to tackle only Scenes I and II with the backlog to be made up later.

5. Homework: complete the journal. Stress that pupils need to keep a record of roughly what each scene involves and to think ahead to what to do in the next scenes.

Lesson 7: Week 3. Character

1. Warm up with a brief rehearsal of Scene II.

2. Model: one group performs, the teacher freezes them at an opportune moment and asks the class 'Whose thoughts do we most want to know?' That pupil then speaks in character about feelings, plans, etc. Choose a couple of other characters then move the scene on and freeze again.

3. Refer to Table 13.1. Discuss how monologues can help develop character and play.

4. Each group runs through a scene of their choice and tries to determine where it would be best to stop the action and introduce a monologue. The relevant character then begins to say what is on their mind. If there is time, perform some of the scenes.

5. Homework: all write a monologue for their character at some midpoint of their play. Look at varieties of monologue.

The importance of the monologues is to act out the emotions of a character. This will mean that pupils have to get into role. For example, a young person is hooked into the drugs scene and has a desperate need for drugs. There is peer pressure on him or her to continue. Where is the money to buy drugs to come from? Steal from the family? How does this feel, is he or she letting them down? How can he or she reconcile this? These thoughts and feelings can be articulated through a pupil taking the role and performing a monologue.

Lessons 8/9: Week 3

1. Work on monologue ideas as the basis for Scene IV, or for the space between Scenes III and IV. Groups need to discuss what they created for homework and what would best suit their piece. If there are difficulties introduce the 'hot seat' (each individual answering questions in character) to the whole class using it to develop character and as a source for new ideas. Ask pupils to return to their groups to use the technique for themselves.

2. Perform some monologues.

3. Move on to Scene V and perform some.

4. Homework: journal.

Lesson 10: Week 4. Acting

This lesson will stand alone and could be used in isolation from the series described here.

Use a pack of playing cards to work on status. Explain how different people have different behavioural status which can be separate from their social status, eg a beggar can have a higher status than a king if the king is timid and the beggar caustic and insistent when asking for money. Line up the whole class except for four volunteers (more of them later). Hand out one card randomly to each person in the line, explaining that the identity of the card *must* be kept secret. Explain that aces have the highest status, with twos and threes the lowest and so on; you might want to remark that the middle numbers are hardest to act.

Now outline a general scenario, for example an advert for chocolate showing an ambassador's reception, and ask each member of the class to adopt a suitable character (ambassador, VIP, butler, cleaner, body guard) and play that role with the status indicated on their card in a large/sometimes unwieldy improvisation;

be prepared to intervene if things get out of hand! All characters should attempt to mingle and discover how they should behave with one another, without mentioning what their status is.

While all this is going on the four volunteers have to try to work out the status value of each person, without asking them or being given any direct indications. They need to keep a record on a single piece of paper. Eventually the volunteers line up the class in what they think is the ascending order of their status and read out what they guessed for each actor. The actor now reveals his or her card and can see how close the 'audience' perception was to their acting status.

- Feedback: often pupils are more comfortable playing either high or low status and there may be discrepancies between the guess and what the actor's status card actually was. There should be discussion on how to act different character types, starting with an understanding of the status of that character and hence the kind of actions, reactions, behaviour, etc they would use in any given circumstances.

- If there is time, repeat the exercise with different volunteers.

- Homework: write up (a) how the status exercise works and (b) what status is and how it can be used in the current performance.

Lessons 11/12: Week 4

1. Let the class know that the last 20 minutes of the lesson will be used for one or two groups to play out their Scenes V and VI. They must work hard in this session.

2. Try to complete scenes V and VI. Pay special attention to acting, ie the status of characters both individually and how they react to one another. Consider how the scenes might look with different status roles.

3. In the last 20 minutes, allow one or two groups to act out their Scenes V and VI. After each performance focus discussion on the believability and success of the acting, using status as a tool for discussion.

4. Homework: journal work.

Lesson 13: Week 5. Analysing acting

1. Introduce and explain the five acting directions:

   – *body position;*

   – *gestures;*

   – *eye contact;*

   – *tone of voice;*

   – *pace of voice.*

   The class should copy basic notes from the board then begin to apply them, eg angry body position, gesture of welcome, different kinds of eye contact and different kinds of messages.

2. Model: take one group and ask them to perform their last complete scene. Using the five acting directions, perhaps one at a time, the rest of the class can begin to offer constructive criticism of the acting and learn what they should look out for in their own and their group's acting. Links can be made with status work and believability.

3. Homework: pupils write up how the five acting directions work and make five suggestions to improve their own acting.

Lessons 14/15: Week 5

1. Brief introduction on what to look out for on the first run through the whole performance, what you learn from doing the whole thing then run through despite any problems; just get to the end.

2. Individual groups discuss any improvements to be made in plot structure and acting. The whole class shares group findings and discusses how to implement suggested improvements.

3. Either have a second run through at this point or hand out lighting and sound cue sheets and give advice on how to prepare technical materials.

4. Homework: journal; reflections on the first run through. Write up lighting and sound cue sheets.

Lesson 16: Week 6. Acting II

This lesson is a *repetition exercise* demonstrating the value of acting with others rather than in isolation. This is another lesson which could stand alone.

1. Divide the class into pairs with A and B facing each other. The As begin by making a simple comment, eg 'Your hair is brown', which Bs repeat in exactly the same tone of voice. Keep the repetition going for several rounds, by which time both partners should be feeling the need to say something different. Now allow As to make one change to the round of repetition when they feel the time is right. Bs then have to repeat the new phrase. One group demonstrates their version. Look at when A decides to change the phrase, what made them do it; was it timing or something else? The idea is to allow the actors to interact intuitively and develop a sense of when the time is right to say their line, rather than come out with it woodenly.

2. The same pairs have a repetition argument beginning with Bs. Each actor is allowed to repeat, with variations in tone, the phrase said by the other. They should continue to use the same phrase until what seems like the right moment to close the argument with a telling change of phrase. Allow pairs to rehearse and show some to the class.

3. Homework: pupils write up how the repetition technique works, what it aims to help actors to do and how it can help the current performance. Pupils to bring in all props and costumes for the next lesson.

Lessons 17/18: Week 6

1. Run through with props and costume.

2. Isolate specific areas for improvement; don't get sidetracked into worrying about the whole thing. Remember to look at

structure, tension, maintaining role, interest in the beginning, reflection, detail in acting, ie status, the five acting directions, thought-tracking, acting with others and not just in your own role.

3. Write down what needs to be improved. Make a realistic list of targets and work to it. This is an opportunity for the teacher to do mid-term assessment. Each group is isolated from other groups and performs the piece to the teacher who will evaluate it with input from the pupils themselves.

4. Homework: journal write-up and building of strategy for the final performance.

Lesson 19: Week 7. The final preparation

1. Rehearse one show with all technical materials in use. Look at practicalities of cue-to-cue, fading, the reality of set and scene changes. Warn of potential hazards.

2. Homework: journal work predicting technical requirements and problems.

Lessons 20/21: Week 7

The last dress rehearsal. Opportunity for more mid-term assessments.

Week 8 – The performance

Following the performance get pupils together to evaluate its strengths and weaknesses.

LINKS WITH CITIZENSHIP

KNOWLEDGE AND UNDERSTANDING ABOUT BECOMING INFORMED CITIZENS

- Pupils learn about the legal and human rights and responsibilities underpinning society and how they relate to citizens and the basic operation of the criminal justice system.

DEVELOPING SKILLS OF ENQUIRY AND COMMUNICATION

- Pupils learn to contribute to group and exploratory class discussion.

DEVELOPING SKILLS OF PARTICIPATION AND RESPONSIBLE ACTION

- Pupils learn to use their imagination to consider other people's experiences and to think about, express and explain views that are not their own.

- They learn to negotiate, decide and take part responsibly in group and school activities.

- They learn to reflect on the process of participating.

CHAPTER 14

DESIGN AND TECHNOLOGY

Design and Technology provides many opportunities for the development of citizenship knowledge. There are chances to explore the commercial world, the effects of design on quality of life and the international exploitation of technology, consumer rights and law.

Skills that can be developed include research (using the Internet, among other sources), debate and discussion, working in collaborative groups on projects, with responsible use of equipment and materials especially around issues of health and safety. In this chapter we include the following activities:

- Key Stage 3

  - *Two or three lessons (extendable) using difference in food habits across the world to explore diversity.*

- Key Stage 4

  - *A term-long project to research the use, financial implications and marketing potential of a clock designed to incorporate a company logo or design theme.*

Design and technology – food/citizenship, Key Stage 3
TITLE: Exploring different food

TIME REQUIRED: Two or three lessons plus preparation. (This can be extended depending upon the time available and the scope of the development of the work.)

AIMS AND OBJECTIVES

For citizenship:

- To recognize and appreciate the racial, cultural and religious diversity of approaches to food across the world.

- To understand the reasons for different countries having different staple foods.

For design and technology – food:

- To look at the different types of food eaten in different countries.

- To make a comparison with British food.

Introduction

Begin with a brainstorm or small group work by pupils to identify the different types of food they have experienced. This will probably result in examples such as Chinese, Indian, Italian, Mexican, Thai, American, etc.

Ask pupils to try to define what are the differences between these styles of food in terms of foods used, preparation methods and ways of serving. Ask pupils to consider why this might be. Explore religious requirements such as halal, kosher or vegetarianism and find examples of this in the food experienced by pupils. Explore the cultivation of staple crops (eg potatoes, rice, wheat) and the raising of food animals (sheep, goats, cattle, pigs) and the availability of wild sources of food, eg fish, deer, and the recent advent of farming these creatures.

Ask pupils to research in cookery books, magazines, by asking parents, relatives and friends for relevant recipes. Ask pupils to investigate the reasons for the origins of these dishes. This will involve some research into the economy and agriculture in the countries involved. www.yumyum.com has hundreds of recipes and can be searched for different categories of food.

Development

If time, and perhaps funds, are available, links could be made with other countries, either through an internationally funded scheme using ICT and video conferencing or less ambitiously through pen friends and the modern languages department.

Another approach might be to involve pupils from ethnic backgrounds that are not English or, if there are not many of these pupils in a school, make contact and exchange with pupils from a school that does have a varied, multicultural population and explore their experience of different foods.

The work could result in the production of a recipe book covering a selection of dishes from different traditions, suitably illustrated using ICT skills.

LINKS WITH CITIZENSHIP

KNOWLEDGE AND UNDERSTANDING ABOUT BECOMING INFORMED CITIZENS

- Pupils learn about the diversity of national, regional, religious and ethnic identities in the United Kingdom and the need for mutual respect and understanding for the different cultural traditions.

- They learn the differences and similarities across the world and how the economic, climatic and cultural differences affect people's eating habits.

DEVELOPING SKILLS OF ENQUIRY AND COMMUNICATION

- Pupils learn to think about topical cultural issues, researching and analysing information using ICT-based sources.

- They learn to contribute to exploratory class discussions.

DEVELOPING SKILLS OF PARTICIPATION AND RESPONSIBLE ACTION

- Pupils learn to use their imagination to look at other peoples' experiences and to think about, express and explain views that are not their own.

- They learn to take part effectively in group, class, school and, potentially, community-based activities.

Design and technology/citizenship, Key Stage 4
TITLE: Clock project

TIME REQUIRED: Series of lessons over one term

AIMS AND OBJECTIVES

For citizenship:

- To research a company and its products.

- To communicate with the company about a design project.

- To learn about the financial implications of such a project.

For design and technology:

- To design a fully working model clock, appropriate for the chosen company to use to promote sales of one of its products.

- To learn about the real environment in which such work is usually undertaken, ie customer requirements, financial constraints, etc.

Introduction

Pupils carry out background research on companies selling products which would lend themselves to the design of a clock, eg a mint sweet in the shape of a ring or a tyre could have a clock face placed in the centre. They choose products which appeal to them, from a design point of view, with brand image or logos which would enhance the appearance and saleability of a clock.

Development

Pupils make contact with their chosen company in the hope of gaining some support for their projects, either financial or the provision of marketing material, or to suggest that someone from the company (an engineer, designer or marketing executive) might visit school to help in the designing phase.

Pupils look into the financial viability of their projects. Could the clocks be mass produced? What would be a realistic cost to the company of a marketing campaign featuring the clock?

Pupils learn the technological skills necessary and complete their working models.

LINKS WITH CITIZENSHIP

KNOWLEDGE AND UNDERSTANDING ABOUT BECOMING INFORMED CITIZENS

- Pupils learn about the commercial exploitation of technology.

- They learn about the role of business and how it uses technology for a wide range of tasks.

- They learn how projects are costed and the economics of business.

DEVELOPING SKILLS OF ENQUIRY AND COMMUNICATION

- Pupils learn to research information and communicate with people from external organizations.

- They research and develop technical skills.

DEVELOPING SKILLS OF PARTICIPATION AND RESPONSIBLE ACTION

- Pupils learn to negotiate with companies and organizations outside the school.

- They learn to operate collectively and individually in a responsible and safe manner over the use of tools and materials.

CHAPTER 15

PHYSICAL EDUCATION

PE and sport promote collaboration, teamwork and the subordination of the self for the team. There are moral dilemmas in sport such as drug-enhanced performance, racism and disability that can be used to promote citizenship and the development of values.

In this section the generic links between the learning in physical education and how it relates to learning about citizenship are described. We feel it is inappropriate to design specific PE activities for this purpose since the learning and skills acquired from PE are essentially those generic skills that will help to underpin other work on citizenship. What we try to show is that within PE activities there are inherent lessons to be drawn about citizenship. What is required is an explicit linking of what is being done or discussed to specific citizenship learning requirements. Some of these links are set out below for both Key Stages 3 and 4.

There is a wide range of direct and indirect links to citizenship that can be drawn from the teaching of physical education. They are linked in each case to one or more of the key strands of citizenship. We set out below, in generic terms, the way that links can be drawn by PE teachers from pupils' work, experience and questions.

Knowledge and understanding about becoming informed citizens

This area can be addressed through an emphasis on the notion of fair play. Games is a compulsory element at Key Stages 3 and 4 in the National Curriculum. In every game activity (which means in a very large part of the PE curriculum) there is the need to compete and to follow rules. In invasion games, where physical contact is possible, fair play is perhaps even more important. This also has implications for the prevention of injury (a health and safety issue) and is also important for social skills. Using pupils as umpires or referees means they are controlling this aspect of fair play and in this way their recognition and awareness of its importance is increased. Awareness and understanding of social and ethnic diversity can be improved through the medium of dance and, for instance, through discussions about racism in sport.

Newspaper and Internet coverage of sports issues can be used as a resource to promote an understanding of the media and how it works to inform and influence opinion. The question of reporting in the media is one that can be discussed at length and can be brought into lessons at appropriate times, eg issues of stereotyping in sports reporting. There is, of course, plenty of evidence of the negative side of sport. The 'lager lout' mentality, the behaviour of football fans abroad has attracted a lot of coverage. Pupils see constant evidence of bad sporting etiquette and poor behaviour by players, athletes, spectators and supporters. The role of the PE teacher is to point these out as examples of bad behaviour. Sometimes role models are not good role models. It is also important, however, to see how the media can have a positive effect upon sport and attitudes towards it. During Wimbledon fortnight, for example, there is the encouragement for people to become involved in tennis. A number of minority sports are covered on television channels and in the sporting press to their benefit.

Moral and social issues can be addressed through discussions on drugs use in sport, on violence on and off the pitch and issues of nationalism and its effects on opinions and behaviour.

Democracy is an issue for electing teams, 'sports player of the year' or similar awards. Democracy may be a question of balance. Within a club situation the best players are chosen as the overriding ambition is to compete and win. Within a school situation it may sometimes be more appropriate to choose players for the team because they turn up for practice every week and give their all. A pupil vote to elect the 'players' player' should encourage those voting to look at *why* they vote – it is not just for the most talented player but for the player who turns out in all weathers, encourages others, is generous in playing as a team member, etc.

Awareness of the role of local and national government can be raised through discussions around funding for sports, sponsorship and lottery cash used to promote sport. Sponsorship also raises a number of issues that can provoke fruitful discussion. On one side there is the desire of young people to possess the best brand-named (and most expensive) trainers and the rather cynical advertising which supports this. On the other is the positive impact of the limiting of cigarette sponsorship to Formula One. This can link in with the health promotion aspect of PE and the implications for the future health and wealth of the country. PE can use much of the current national research into health and health related issues. Constantly, throughout all teaching, PE can promote a healthy life-style.

A greater awareness of international issues can be raised through study of the rules, protocols and mechanics of student, Commonwealth and Olympic Games. Moral and social issues can also be raised. Within sport there is the whole issue of sporting etiquette – the 'unwritten rule'. In football, for example, if someone is injured a player from the opposing side kicks the ball off the pitch. The following throw in is taken by a member of the injured player's team and by convention is thrown straight to a member of the opposite side. This can provoke all sorts of debate.

As far as international issues are concerned, there are the benefits of international sports, the experience of travelling to events, the links with different races, the growing understanding of other cultures and the development of strong friendships across the cultures. There are also occasionally major problems such as the boycotting of sporting events over a political issue. The morality of sport being used to make a political point is one that can be hotly debated. Gender issues are also important. Nationally there is a large problem with the falling participation levels of teenage girls in PE, with resultant implications for long-term health and fitness; it is a responsibility of the PE department to plan teaching aimed at keeping this group motivated. Against this there may be the exact reverse in that young girls can become 'training crazy' and this may result in eating disorders.

Developing skills of enquiry and communication

PE is a good opportunity to raise lessons of co-operation and group interaction both on and off the field, working as a team, responding to the coach, the role of the captain, the giving and receiving of advice. There are opportunities for research, using a variety of media, into social and moral issues related to sport (for example, cheating, use of performance-enhancing drugs and racism).

Such research can lead to group discussions which give pupils the opportunity to express and justify their opinions.

Developing skills of participation and responsible action

Pupils can learn to participate responsibly as part of a group in sporting and similar activities and, for older pupils, to help and support younger pupils through coaching. Representative sport, whether as a participant or as a spectator, for the year or the school (and more advanced opportunities for the more able) provides plenty of opportunity to reflect upon and discuss the nature of participation, responsible behaviour and how changes can be brought about. There may be many reasons for participation – the enjoyment of taking part, to win, for social reasons or for rewards. Discussion can centre on these reasons.

Pupils can be encouraged to consider the experience of others. Imagine what it is like not to be good at a sport. Work can be done to help understand the problems faced by the less able or those who find it more difficult for some reason, for example the left-handed tennis player.

PE also encourages responsible action. Questions of conflicting loyalties to school and club can arise. What if there is a clash of fixtures? Where do priorities lie? How is this situation dealt with?

CHAPTER 16

BUSINESS STUDIES (KEY STAGE 4)

Business studies provides many opportunities for the study of citizenship. Many business studies topics are themselves directly related to issues that need to be addressed in the citizenship curriculum.

Issues such as poverty, the globalization of business, the roles and responsibilities of employers and employees, trade in the EU and the way that the economy functions are clearly overlapping in the citizenship curriculum and programme of work with work that may already be going on in business studies.

Exploring all these issues will give a wide perspective on business both at the micro-level of the rights and responsibilities of employers and employees and at the macro-level with the impact of global business on people of developing countries as well as everything in between.

In this chapter we include a series of four lessons exploring poverty and business.

Business studies/citizenship, Key Stage 4
TITLE: Poverty and business

TIME REQUIRED: A series of four lessons plus preparation

RESOURCES REQUIRED: *Nuffield/BP Business Studies for GCSE* (1996) by S Barnes *et al*. A video focusing on poverty.

AIMS AND OBJECTIVES

For citizenship and business studies:

- To understand the difference between developed and developing worlds.

- To understand how poverty differs between the developed and developing worlds.

- To investigate poverty in the developed and developing worlds.

- To investigate how poverty in the developed and developing worlds is affected by economic forces.

- To understand the meaning of absolute and relative poverty.

- To use the Internet to research and collate data on the distribution of wealth in the UK and world-wide.

- To understand how poverty is linked to business activities.

- To explore how one industry links the economies of two countries.

Activity: meaning of poverty

Ask pupils to brainstorm on the meaning of poverty and who is poor. Then ask them to read pages 192–193 of *Nuffield/BP Business and Economics for GCSE*. This section is entitled 'A wealth of difference' and asks who are the winners and who are the losers? This gives factual material (including a picture) relating to four different people:

- Pappathy who earns 30p a day for picking coffee.

- A minor member of royalty choosing a dress for a party before being driven there by the chauffeur.

- Josh who lives on the streets of New York and who can't claim benefits.

- Jack, a founder of Littlecomfurt Computer Software, who receives in excess of $5 million per week.

Ask pupils to discuss their reactions to the information and answer three questions:

1. Suppose each of these people were given an extra £100. What do you think they would spend it on?

2. How would it affect the work they do?

3. How would the way they spend the £100 affect other people living near them?

Then ask pupils to discuss the extremes of wealth and poverty and introduce the idea of a rich world and a poor world. This leads on to an analysis of data on earnings in different parts of the world. Data given in the source text includes:

- International wages, 1992. Source: World Bank, *World Development Report*, Oxford University Press, 1995.

- Wages for five groups (engineer, skilled industrial worker, bus driver, construction worker, female unskilled textile worker) in different countries. Source: Union Bank of Switzerland, 1994.

Develop the discussion of data into work on how income is shared. Data in the text is from the Central Statistical Office, *Social Trends*, HMSO, 1995. This information can be used to reveal that the world is not equal in terms of wealth, and should prompt discussion of whether we wish to make it more equal, what might happen if it became more equal and how we could help to make it more equal.

You may wish to research your own data and statistics for this work. The Office of National Statistics is a useful source of such material. They publish a National Trends Pocketbook and their Web site is at www.statistics.gov.uk

Activity: tea industry

Ask pupils to begin an examination of the tea industry by conducting a survey (which could be within the group or wider) looking at the amount of tea drunk and the brands bought. Share the results.

Ask pupils to read pages 194–195 of *Nuffield/BP Business Studies for GCSE*. This section is a continuation of the work on 'A wealth of difference' and develops the question 'Who are the winners and who are the losers?' It gives information relating to the following:

- The UK tea market where four companies (Brooke Bond, Tetley's, Hillsdown and Co-operative Wholesale) supply three-quarters of all tea drunk. Source: The Tea Council.

- Tea consumption around the world (cups per person per year) in 1993. Source: The Tea Council.

- World exports of tea. Source: The Tea Council.

- Factual evidence (including pictures) is also given relating to earning a living from picking tea in Bangladesh and in India.

Ask pupils to produce a chart using the data on stakeholders in the tea industry.

Activity: absolute vs. relative poverty

Conduct a discussion on absolute and relative poverty. Notes and examples to be given. Then watch a video looking at the effects of poverty in the UK. The video around which the lesson was originally based was programme 4 of the BBC series *A Labour of Love*, first broadcast c.1993, and is called 'Poverty'. An alternative would be from another BBC series on the history of the Welfare State, called *The New Jerusalem*, first broadcast in 1995. Programme 4 – 'For Richer for Poorer' – is about unemployment and starts with some relevant information on poverty. Both would be part of the BBC Broadcast Archives of programmes and as they are educational will be available for purchase, although you cannot access details on the Internet but have to contact your local BBC office for details.

Alternatively, extracts could be used from *Cathy Come Home* or *Poor Cow*. Every film available in the UK can be obtained from MovieMail. Telephone 01432 262910 Fax: 01432 262913. Web site: www.moviem.co.uk. e-mail: enquiries@moviem.co.uk

It is also possible to encourage pupils to watch current TV 'soaps' to give them ideas about poverty.

Ask pupils to complete the 'Poverty Worksheet' overleaf.

Activity: fair shares?

Use pages 185–186 of *Nuffield/BP Business and Economics for GCSE Teachers' Resource Pack* (1996) edited by N. Wall. The exercise is called 'Fair shares?'

POVERTY WORKSHEET

(All references are to **Nuffield/BP Business and Economics for GCSE**, 1996)

Poverty exists throughout the world but today is more extreme in the developing world. What examples of poverty can you think of in the UK?

1. **Causes of poverty.** Many of these are linked with business and economic activity, eg unemployment, low wages, poor working conditions. Find and describe examples of poverty from your textbook (Unit 6).

2. The video shows the effect of poverty in the UK. As you watch it make a note of the ways in which poor people try to meet their basic needs and the various ways in which they overcome their financial difficulties.

3. After you have watched the video try to identify reasons why life is better for many people now. Think especially about the effect of business activity.

These are difficult questions and no-one knows all of the answers. These sections in the textbook will help you:

'Who gains from growth?'	Page 124
'Can the government rule the roller coaster?'	Page 116
'What is growth?'	Page 156
'Going for growth?'	Page 158
'A wealth of difference'	Page 193
'Who are winners and losers?'	Page 194
'Down the slippery slope'	Page 196

KNOWLEDGE AND UNDERSTANDING ABOUT BECOMING INFORMED CITIZENS

- Pupils learn about how the economy functions including the role of business and financial services.

- They learn about the importance of a free press and the media's role in society, including the Internet, in providing information and affecting opinion.

- They learn about the wider issues and challenges of global interdependence and responsibility.

DEVELOPING SKILLS OF ENQUIRY AND DEBATE

- Pupils learn to research a topical political, moral or social issue using different sources, including Internet sources, gaining awareness of the use of statistics.

- They form, express and justify a personal opinion about these issues.

- They contribute to group and exploratory class discussions.

DEVELOPING SKILLS OF PARTICIPATION AND RESPONSIBLE ACTION

- Pupils learn to use their imagination to consider other people's experiences and to think about, express and explain views that are not their own.

- They take part responsibly in group and school activities.

It looks at 'Who gets the most?', the wages/salaries received by a range of people (£120 per week to £900,000 per year) and suggests listing the whole working population of Britain in order of income. That list should then be divided into five equal parts, with about 5.8 million people in each part.

Pupils are then asked to estimate the earnings of people in each fifth. (Government statistics can be obtained to provide this information.) Pupils are then given five jobs and asked to place them in each fifth. These are a staff nurse in an NHS hospital, an airline pilot, a hairdresser, a branch bank manager and a skilled welder.

Ask pupils to complete Activity 76. This uses data and the Nuffield/BP programme which accompanies the text.

REFERENCES

Barnes, S, Lines, D, Wales, J and Wall, N (1996) *Nuffield/BP Business Studies and Economics for GCSE*, Collins Educational, London

BECTa (1999) *Superhighways Safety: Childrens' Safe Use of the Internet*, Department for Education and Employment (DfEE), Sudbury

Bowen, A and Pallister, J (1999) *Understanding GCSE Geography*, Heinemann Educational, London

Brien, A, Brien, S and Dobson, S (1993) *Projekt Deutsch, Book 4*, Oxford University Press, Oxford

Briggs, I, Goodman-Stephens, B and Rogers, P (1992) *Route Nationale, Book 1*, Thomas Nelson, London

Brown, L (producer) (1980) *Skyscrapers and Slums*, BBC Television, London

Central Statistical Office (1995) *Social Trends*, HMSO, London

Clarke, S and Thompson, M (1996) *Buddhism: A New Approach*, Hodder and Stoughton Educational, London

Cunliffe, B (1993) *The Roman Baths, A View over 200 Years*, Batsford/English Heritage, London

Duffy, CA ed (1996) *Stopping for Death*, Viking Poetry (Penguin), London

Ebborn, A and Alcorn, M (1990) *Squeeze Words Hard*, Longman, London

Fuller, S ed (1991) *The Poetry of Protest*, BBC Consumer Publishing, London

NEAB Anthology (1996), Heinemann Educational, London

Nuffield Foundation (1998) *Beyond 2000: Science Education for the Future, the Report of a Seminar Series*, London

Ofsted (1998) *Annual Report 1998*. Office for Standards in Education, London

Organisation for Economic Co-operation and Development (OECD) (1999) *Environmental Data Compendium*, OECD, Paris

Owen Cole, W (1991) *Moral Issues in Six Religions*, Heinemann Educational, London

Qualifications and Curriculum Authority (QCA)/DfEE (1998) *Education for Citizenship and the Teaching of Democracy in Schools* (The Crick Report), QCA, London

QCA/DfEE (1999a) *Citizenship: The National Curriculum for England Key Stages 3–4*, QCA, London

QCA/DfEE (1999b) *Preparing for Working Life*, QCA, London

Stephenson, P Ed (1982) *Handbook of World Development: A Guide to the Brandt Report*, Holmes and Meier, New York

Thompson, M (1998) *The Buddhist Experience*, Hodder and Stoughton Educational, London

Walkington, H (1999) *Theory into Practice; Global Citizenship Education*, Geographical Association, Sheffield

Wall, N ed (1996) *Nuffield/BP Business Studies for GCSE, Teachers Resource Pack*, Collins Educational, London

Waugh, D (1991) *Key Geography Connections*, Stanley Thornes, Cheltenham

World Bank (1995) *World Development Report*, Oxford University Press, Oxford

Wilde, O (1898) *The Ballad of Reading Gaol*

Wright, C (1997) *Buddhism for Today*, Oxford University Press, Oxford

USEFUL CONTACTS AND WEB SITES

British Education and Communications Technology Agency: Virtual Teacher Centre Web site is a huge resource for teachers on a wide range of subjects vtc.ngfl.gov.uk/vtc/library/pub.html

Christian Aid (for the Trading Game): PO Box 100, London SE1 7RT. www.christian-aid.org.uk

Community Service Volunteers: this organization works with schools and colleges to enable young people to become active citizens through practical projects addressing community needs. www.csv.org.uk

The Council for Education in World Citizenship: an independent educational organization specializing in creating partnerships with local, national and global organizations to develop active learning opportunities in citizenship. www.cewc.org.uk

Department for Education and Employment (DfEE): Sanctuary Buildings, Great Smith Street, London SW1P 3BT

The Hansard Society: promotes knowledge about parliament and government. It can provide high quality material for mock elections in schools www.hansardsociety.org.uk

The Institute for Citizenship: the institute's aim is to promote citizenship by developing innovative projects for citizenship education. www.citizen.org.uk

Learning Partnership West: produce an excellent Work Experience Log Book. Contact: Jill King, Work Experience Manager (tel: 0117 987 2444)

National Curriculum Web site: www.nc.uk.net

National Healthy School Standard: a standard for schools to use to review their whole school provision of citizenship and PSHE. www.wiredforhealth.gov.uk

http://citfou.org.uk is the Citizenship Foundation site

http://citizen.org.uk is the Institute for Citizenship site

http://vtc.ngfl.gov.uk/vtc/library/pub.html is a site of the British Education and Communications Technology Agency and Department for Education site with a useful guidance document about schools' Internet usage

www.bbc.co.uk/education is BBC Online with linked access to a range of educational Web sites

www.charter88.org.uk is a site campaigning for 'a modern and fair democracy in the UK'

www.citizen21.org.uk is 'an online resource for educators' from which resources can be downloaded

www.eun.org offers a civics section in its 'Virtual School' with a discussion forum and occasional contacts with MEPs

www.fco.gov.uk Foreign and Commonwealth Office site with information on studying overseas cultures

www.NISS.ac.uk/world/schools.html provides a huge collated list of sources of information for schools

www.oneworld.org described by the Crick Report as an excellent source dedicated to promoting human rights and sustainable development

www.webwombat.com provides details of how to contact over 10,000 worldwide newspapers for up-to-the-minute comment on events. You can search by individual country/by subject matter etc

www.wotw.org.uk is an organization promoting international school links

INDEX